Please

[signature]

The Consumer's Guide to Health Savings Accounts (HSAs)

Health Savings Accounts,
The powerful consumer-directed tool
that lowers health care costs and builds tax-free savings.

Learn what HSAs can do for you!

by JoAnn Mills Laing

Foreword by David F. Durenberger,
Chair, National Institute of Health Policy
U.S. Senator (R-MN, 1978-1995)

Brick Tower Press
New York

Warning and Disclaimer

Information contained in this book is included with the understanding that the author and the publisher are not engaged in rendering legal, accounting or other professional services. If legal advice or other expert assistance is required, the services of a competent professional person should be sought. Every effort has been made to make this book as complete and accurate as possible, but no warranty of fitness is implied. The information provided is on an "as is" basis. The author and the publisher shall have neither liability nor responsibility to any person or entity with respect to any loss or damages arising from the information contained in this book.

Dedication

To OSO, Innovator

Laing, JoAnn Mills
The Consumer's Guide to Health Savings Accounts (HSAs)
Includes Index
ISBN 1-883283-46-9

Library of Congress Control Number: 2005920570
First Edition, March 2005

Contents

This chapter will help you get familiar with the basics of health savings accounts and how they can help you save money—starting now—regardless of your employment situation.
>   -What's in it for you?
>   -Who qualifies?
>   -What's covered?
>   -Lower health care costs for businesses and individuals
>   -Health care premium costs
>   -Tax relief for individuals
>   -An "above-the-line" tax write-off
>   -Evolution of an idea
>   -Why flexible spending accounts are finished
>   -An advantage for early movers

In this chapter, you'll learn how you can qualify for an HSA. Worksheets and quizzes will give you an idea of how much you might be able to save.

-What types of businesses qualify?
-A business needs how many employees to qualify?
-How do individuals or individual workers become
      eligible for an HSA?
-Other allowable insurance plans
-Who will not qualify?
-HSAs as part of your employee health benefits package
-Who will benefit the most from HSAs?
-How much will it cost?
-Myth: "I can't afford health insurance!"
-Calculating costs and savings for the self-employed

A qualifying high-deductible health plan is the essential first step to opening an HSA. So how do you go about finding one? Whether you're running a business or working for one, there's a plan out there for you. This chapter discusses what to look for and why, the government regulations that determine which plans qualify, and other considerations to keep in mind.

-Why a high-deductible plan?
-Not all high-deductible plans qualify
-No copays, but some coinsurance
-Out-of-pocket maximums for coinsurance
-Does my existing HMO or PPO qualify?
-How do I buy a high-deductible insurance policy?
      -Individual or group coverage?
      -Individual or family plan?
      -Employees with poor health histories
      -Employees with families
-Finding a vendor for qualified high-deductible plans
      -Using rating services
      -State licensing agencies
      -Why choose a smaller firm at all?
      -Can I be rejected?
      -What if I have a "pre-existing condition"?
      -Age and residency requirements

-Finding a policy provider for your small business
>-Should you switch providers?
>-Dealing with resistance
>-Comparing high-deductible plans
>-Common exclusions
>-Guaranteed renewability
>-Coverage out of state
>-Care management policies
>-Customer service
>-Before you sign on the dotted line . . .
>-Key financial considerations for any policy plan
>-What to look for: A checklist

Now that you've opened a qualifying health insurance policy, it's time to start saving money. This chapter gives you a look at HSA vendors and criteria for choosing among them, legal requirements, the paperwork you can expect to fill out, and the rest of the process.

>-Who offers HSAs today?
>>-Who can be an "Account Custodian"?
>>-Can you be your own custodian?
>-What to look for
>>-FDIC Insurance—a must
>>-A track record
>>-State regulations
>>-Using an online institution
>-Opening the account
>-IRS reporting requirements and your privacy
>-About the paperwork

HSAs can be a powerful savings vehicle, but only if you know how to use them. This chapter will help you develop a savings strategy for your family or your small business. A contribution calculator and a discussion of relevant taxes will help you get the most out of your account.

-Determining your contribution limit
  -The contribution calculator
  -Special rules for those over 55
-Maximizing your contributions
-Penalties on excess contributions
-Employee vs. employer contributions: Pros, cons, and
  useful compromises
  -Reportability
  -The non-discrimination rule
  -The portability factor

Sooner or later you're going to need some of your HSA money. Read this chapter before you spend a penny to make sure you're not incurring avoidable tax penalties.

-Sticker shock: Adjusting to pay-as-you-go health care
-A breakthrough: Who is covered?
  -Where copays are covered: The exceptional exception
-Payment mechanisms
-What's deductible and considered a qualifying medical
  expense?
  -What does NOT qualify?
  -What's debatable?
-Choosing your own doctors, and meeting your deductibles
-Getting the PPO discount
-Becoming a better health care consumer
-The rollover
-Financial cushion? Or money mattress?
-Preventative care
-Long term care
-Keeping track and correcting mistakes
-Nine ways to get the most out of your HSA dollars

- Tax exemption and tax deferrals for individuals
  - Tax treatment of earnings
  - Withdrawal penalties
  - Death benefits
  - Tax rule on rollovers
  - Rules for reporting premium costs and HSA
    contributions
  - HSAs and the form 1040
- If you're self-employed: Finding business deductions in the
  tax code
  - Tax exemption and business expense deductions for
    the self-employed
  - Sole proprietors with employees
  - Administrative tax credit
  - Where it goes on the schedule C
  - Rules for unincorporated partnerships
  - LLCs and LLPs
  - C and S corporations
  - Working with the W-2

- Integrating HSAs with other benefits
  - The mighty IRA
  - How HSAs may work with HRAs or FSAs
  - How HSAs work with COBRA

- The COBRA waiver
   -How HSAs work with unemployment benefits
   -Retirement issues and social security

Now that you know what to look for and how to look for it, use
these lists and estimated schedules to keep your plan on track.
   -Checklist for individuals: Enrolling in a new health benefit
      plan
   -Checklist for the self-employed and the small-business
      owner: Launching a new health benefit plan
   -The HRA "three-step"

   A. Setting up your payroll for HSAs
   B. More on employee benefits
   C. Checklist: Communicating the program to employees
   D. Converting an existing benefits plan for the HSA program

Foreword

The advent of the Health Savings Account (HSA) and the accompanying high-deductible health plan is a little bit like going back to the future. For a generation of people who have been raised on managed care and provider networks, the HSA represents a new way of accessing health care. For others this is a return to an old way of ensuring access to major medical insurance and self-managing health care expenses.   The difference between yesterday's major medical and today's consumer-driven health care (CDHC) is the exponential growth in the cost of medical expenses.

For both, JoAnn Laing's book *The Consumer's Guide to Health Savings Accounts* is an excellent source of useful information and guidance. It also provides a vocabulary with which to navigate the sea of options that individuals will face as consumers are asked to take more responsibility for their choices of insurance and of health and medical services. HSAs offer a mechanism for those who want more control over their health care expenses and Ms. Laing does a good job unpacking the toolkit to help the reader understand and use a sometimes complex product.

Everyone is paying attention to HSAs and for good reason. As a tax policy, HSA's will be effective in moving people towards a save now, spend later mentality for health care. And, with more walk-around health care money in their pockets that is theirs to spend—or save—employees may become more savvy purchasers of health care goods and services. Providers will necessarily become more sensitive to consumer demands, and employers will have a more useful role to play in partnering for wellness.

In order for the HSA to have its hoped-for impact on health care costs, it is up to every health care stakeholder to participate in changing the system. Consumers who buy an HSA and high-deductible plan will indeed be charting their own course. But they will still be at the mercy of a complicated $1.7 trillion-a-year medical system built on a "trust me, don't question me" philosophy. This is a system that is only barely and reluctantly beginning to make an effort to provide useable and effective information about health care quality, service, and price.

With an HSA in hand and the freedom to "self manage" one's health care, the consumer will find the health care system to be not unlike a Super Target or WalMart Superstore. Thousands of choices—choices of providers, services, products, technologies, information sources all packaged to attract your attention and your buying power—but limited information about whether those choices are good for your health. There will be a tendency to walk right past the "produce counter" and the expensive "natural foods aisle" in favor of the cheaper, "ready-to-eat products" that the health care industry has to offer. But you don't want to skip what's good for you in favor of what's affordable.

What most of us want for ourselves and our family is a productive, ongoing relationship with a physician and with a clinical care system that delivers reliable, effective care coordination, an integrated information network, and a system-wide commitment to quality and safety. In other words, we don't shop for price alone. We shop for value— the right service or treatment at the right place at the right time.

health care providers have a responsibility to respond to this new way of doing business. Patients will come armed with more questions, more information—some good and some bad—and a real interest in paying only for necessary and appropriate care. Providers are the ones who can answer the question: What does the system need to look like in order for a consumer to know whether they are buying coordinated care based on value not just on price? As Dr. Don Berwick, a nationally recognized champion of health care quality improvement says, "Let's make the organizational leaders responsible to produce organizations to give us the care we're paying for."

Employers have been crushed by the continuing cost growth for their employees' health care benefits. HSAs offer a welcome alternative to eliminating health care coverage altogether, or worse, being forced to tap the international market in search of cheaper labor. But they let no employer off the hook. Employers and employer coalitions make a difference. American employers in a global market have more at stake in a productive, healthy workforce than in cheap labor. Only when employers partner with employees and community health resources can they assure this edge in the market.

Employers have a significant amount of "face time" with employees and can be an influential partner in health and wellness efforts. As an agent of their employees, employers must work with their benefits administrator and the provider community at large to ensure that what they are delivering is real choice. Not choice among a random selection of low-priced, fragmented services, but choice among competing systems of integrated care and service delivery—a choice of performers not producers.

As a major policy initiative that reflects a move to the "ownership" society, the HSA represents a substantial shift in the way American's think about how we finance needed medical services. Built solely on the foundation of private insurance, the sustainability of the HSA is jeopardized. It is an attractive option for those who use the system on a limited basis and whose health care costs are minimal. It's a way out of the pricier, sicker risk pool that many are forced to pay into today. It's also an incentive to stay healthy and save. By allowing those who are healthy and stay healthy to opt out, the payers who employ or insure the cost of care for those who have complex, expensive illnesses will be challenged to control premium growth.

We used to think about insurance in terms of community rating, literally the idea of healthy young able-bodied workers easing access for older and sicker Americans. Most industrialized countries take care of the sick and disabled through "social insurance." And in many of those countries social insurance is delivered through a single payer—the government. Here in the United States we built a pluralistic system of private and social insurance tied to employment and wages. We are now faced with an unraveling of the system that has provided health care coverage for the majority of our citizens, and unless we also reform the private insurance system to make sure that it remains affordable and available to every American, the premise of CDHC will come to naught.

As a nation, we cannot depend on the informed consumer and CDHC as the only cure for what ails our system. Such useful tools as the HSA must be coupled with real system reform—both delivery and financing reform—from the bottom up, from the inside out. National tax policy will not change the way health care is delivered in your community. All stakeholders need to work together to eliminate misuse, under use, and overuse of health care services and insist that performance, not high-volume productivity is what we want to pay for.

Read this book. Ms. Laing will help you make the most of the HSA to benefit you and your family. Spend wisely, gather information, be prepared for catastrophic illness, and choose performers, not services. Lean on your employer and health plan to help you navigate the system. But most importantly, make the most of your relationship with your provider as the key to "self" managing your health care.

David Durenberger
Chair, National Institute of Health Policy
U.S. Senator (R-MN, 1978-1995)

Preface

The rising cost of health care is a major force affecting business and individuals. Health care insurance premiums have risen by double digits over the past decade, forcing many individuals to join the ranks of the uninsured, and many businesses to discontinue health insurance benefits. Four main factors have caused the increased costs of health care services- Technology, Prescription Drugs, Defensive Medicine and Utilization. Previous attempts to control these costs have failed due in large part to a flaw in the health insurance system.

The problem or flaw is a disconnect between the patient, the provider and the true cost of health care services. This has led to lack of consumerism and individual responsibility in the health care industry and has dramatically changed the way health care is provided in the United States.

Health Savings Accounts or HSA's became law as part of the Medicare Modernization Act of 2003. The enactment of HSA's, in my opinion, is the greatest change to our health care system since the development of the Medicare program. HSA's reconnect the patient and provider with the cost of health care services. HSA's empower the individual to make appropriate health care decisions in concert with their medical provider, they restore the doctor-patient relationship.

HSA's are combined with a high deductible health plan (HDHP) and have replaced Archer MSA's as the cornerstone of a new era in health care insurance- Consumer Directed Healthcare. HSA's decrease health care insurance premiums on average 25%-50%. Health savings accounts and their predecessor MSA's have lowered health care costs 30%-50% by changing the behavior of the patient and provider. Employers and employees can use the premium savings to fund the health savings account. These funds are used to pay for qualified health care expenses tax-free and can be withdrawn at retirement for income tax-defferred. The greatest benefit of HSA's is that unused monies in the account roll over from year to year and earn interest. Experts predict that 25% of Americans will have an HSA by 2007 and up to 50% by 2010. The greatest obstacle to health savings accounts is- Education. Many of us have never heard of HSA's, MSA's, FSA's, HRA's and CDHP's. This health care alphabet soup can at times be confusing and disheartening. This book provides valuable information on HSA's and the new era of health care benefits. While many think that they can't understand these new terms, I will remind you that none of us knew what an HMO, PPO, "gatekeeper" and pre-certification were prior to 1970. These terms became household words because we learned them when they became our form of health care insurance.

As a physician, I believe that Health Savings Accounts are the answer to our health care insurance crisis. Enjoy this book and its valuable information. Welcome to the New Era of Healthcare Insurance!

Dr. William J. West
First HSA, Inc.

Introduction

What everyone needs to know about paying for health care.

Who Needs this Book?

* Parents
* New graduates entering the workforce for the first time
* Employees of large corporations
* Employees of small and medium businesses
* People without jobs
* The self-employed
* Entrepreneurs
* Anyone concerned about retirement income
* Anyone who needs health care and wants to know how to pay less for it.

Whether you need it once a day, once a month, or once a year, you can't escape it: you need health care. That means you need to pay for it. And - if you're like the vast majority of Americans - that means you're spending a lot more money on it than you were even three or four years ago.

If you've always worked for relatively large companies, you may not have given much thought to health care until recently.

For the past several decades, most companies have offered their health care benefits under a system called "managed care," in which employees paid a small set fee for most medical services and the company shouldered the rest of the costs. Managed care, in effect, means you don't have to think much about your health care.

Under managed care, you don't have to know what a prescription really costs, or why. You don't have to know which hospitals are the most efficient at a given procedure - and indeed, in a restrictive network-based plan, you probably don't have the freedom to choose between hospitals anyway. Under managed care, all you really need to know is this: As long as you follow the plan's rules, you'll be okay.

Unfortunately, that means many Americans are dangerously ignorant about one of the most important parts of their lives. Why "dangerously"? Well, as you've probably heard, for several years health care costs have been growing at astronomical rates - outpacing both inflation and wage growth several times over. So far, people in employer-sponsored managed care plans have been shielded from the worst of the cost increases, because under those plans the employers have been picking up most of the tab.

But, companies can't afford to keep doing that. Some - especially small businesses - have been forced to stop offering health insurance altogether. Many others are changing the way they offer health care, shifting more of the costs to employees, and asking employees to take more personal and financial responsibility for their own health. It's time to ask yourself: When you have to get more care on your own dollar, not your employer's, do you know enough about health care - and health coverage - to spend those dollars wisely?

Chances are you haven't heard much about one of the most innovative new ways to make smart financial decisions about your health - Health Savings Accounts, or HSAs. This book will bring you up to speed.

Now, if you're self-employed, or you work for a small business, probably none of this seems like much of a shock. You've probably had to pay for most or all of your health care coverage for years, so you knew right away when costs started rising. But you might not know all you could about some brand-new programs you can use to save substantial amounts of money on these costs.

And what if you're one of the 45 million Americans without health insurance? New legislation means you might be able to afford it after all—and possibly get a big tax break in the process.

Whether you work for yourself or a multinational corporation, chances are you like to save money on health care and hang onto more of your income. But first, you have to know how.

This book will show you how to get the most out of the brand-new Health Savings Accounts (HSAs):
- Real-life examples of people in a variety of situations show you how to turn this new product to your greatest advantage.
- Checklists help you make sure you're covering all the bases.
- Calculators and worksheets assist you in tailoring your benefits to your specific situation.
- References - including a glossary of health-care terms and several online resources - help you become a better-informed consumer of health care.

In addition, the appendix offers small business owners some useful information about incorporating HSAs into existing workplace programs.

Finally, remember that HSAs are brand-new - less than a year old, as of this writing. Though we have some pretty good ideas of how they'll play out in the real world, no one knows exactly what will happen. The best thing you can do is educate yourself.

What is an HSA and What's in it for You?

1

A Health Savings Account (HSA) is pretty much what it sounds like: an account that helps you save money on health care. HSAs were designed to help people "self-manage" medical expenses to reduce their costs for health care.

Health Savings Accounts help you save money on unavoidable expenses *and* build investment savings for your retirement.

The HSA program has two parts: a high-deductible health insurance policy; and a trust account or trust fund similar to those used for an IRA, Keogh, or 401(k). The trust account is a tax-free health spending account that, after its first tax year, becomes a tax-advantaged savings account. Dollars put into the account can be withdrawn instantly for qualified medical expenses as needed; any dollars remaining can be rolled over for spending in future years, or invested to accumulate savings for health needs after retirement. It offers individuals a *tax-advantaged way* to accumulate savings for medical expenses. For the self-employed, and for individuals employed by corporations of all sizes, HSAs represent a breakthrough strategy that can offer modest tax relief, lower health care costs and increase retirement savings for future health care needs.

HSAs operate in much the same manner as IRA, Keogh and 401(k) plans, with several important differences. The most important difference is that money placed into an HSA can be withdrawn at any time, before or after retirement, if the money is used for medical care expenses. What constitutes a medical expense is pretty basic. Getting treatment for your broken leg is okay. Having your teeth whitened is not.

What's In It for You?

What's so special about HSAs? See if you could benefit from any of these features. An HSA is:

- A way to save money on health care.

You may have heard about tax-advantaged Flexible Spending Accounts; HSAs are less restrictive and easier to use. There's no getting around it: sooner or later you'll have to spend money on health care. But an HSA might help you spend less.

- A tax saver.

Not only does an HSA let you cover your medical costs tax-free, but your contributions to the account may nudge you into a lower tax bracket — so you could save on your tax bill, not just your health care costs.

- Portable.

HSAs can travel with you from job to job. You always have a right to 100 percent of the money in your account. With health care costs skyrocketing, many employees are trapped in what's known as "job lock" — they're unsatisfied with their current job, but scared to leave because they depend on employer-provided health insurance. HSAs can help to lessen that dependence.

- A source of investment income.

HSAs are designed so that you can always withdraw money when you need it. But the money you *don't* withdraw has the potential to grow and accumulate interest tax-free.

Who Qualifies?

Any taxpayer under the age of 65 can open an HSA account, provided that he or she has also contracted for a high-deductible insurance policy. The self-employed or those employed by others can participate. Spouses or dependents covered by other insurance may not be able to participate (see Chapter 2).

How Much Can You Save?

The eventual worth of your HSA depends on a number of factors, such as:
- Your age when you open the account
- How much you contribute each year (your maximum permissible contribution may vary, depending on your circumstances)
- How much you withdraw each year to spend on qualifying medical expenses
- Whether you roll another account balance into your HSA
- Interest rates and investment growth
- Your age when you begin using the account for retirement income

Let's look at what happens if you contribute $2,600 annually and take no withdrawals. Let's say the money compounds at 5 percent:

After 10 years, the account would be worth $44,000.
After 20 years, the account would be worth $101,000.
After 30 years, the account would be worth $190,000.
After 40 years, the account would be worth $334,000.*

* Source of projections: The Employee Benefit Research Institute.

Remember, actual numbers will be different due to a variety of influences.

Now, obviously, these circumstances are exceptional. Even if you're in excellent health, chances are you'll have a reason or two to withdraw some of your HSA money. Everyone needs health care sometimes.

The real lesson of these numbers? Start saving early. Look again at the difference between the account after 30 years and the account after 40 years.

Here's a different way to look at it: The first number—$190,000—is what you would have at age 65 if you didn't start saving until age 35. (Again, these are sample numbers only, and they assume ideal conditions.) The second number—$334,000—is what you would have at age 65 if you started saving at age 25. That's a difference of $144,000!

And how about this? If you started at age 25, you'd only have to save $26,000—$2,600 every year for 10 years—to get that $144,000. The earlier you start, the harder your money works for you. You might think you can't afford to save anything right now—but the real question is, Can you afford *not* to?

What's Covered?

Dollars put into an HSA account can be used for any medical expense that qualifies as a "medical expense," as defined in section 213(d) of the U.S. tax code (see Chapter 6, page 114 or visit www.irs.gov for a complete listing of 2004 qualified expenses). Many expenses usually not covered under a standard health insurance policy do qualify here and can be paid for out of the HSA.

What can it pay for?

Here's just a sample of what you can purchase tax-free with funds from your HSA:

- Dental and optical care, including glasses and contact lenses
- COBRA health care continuation when you leave a job
- Long-term care insurance for family members
- Fertility treatments, birth control prescriptions, well-baby care
- Physical therapy, chiropractic care, psychoanalysis, acupuncture

---

Because the HSA is tied to a high-deductible health insurance policy, you will "pay as you go" for medical care, using your tax-free HSA dollars, until you spend up to the deductible. Once the deductible is met, the health insurance pays for most of your medical expenses for the rest of the year. You may choose your own doctor and level of care. By themselves, HSAs are savings vehicles — not insurance policies — so they don't restrict your access to coverage or your choice of providers.

In theory, HSAs allow working people to enjoy a broader range of care services, without having to worry about losing everything in an accident or serious illness. And if they don't spend the money, they get to save it and invest it, or use it in later years for health care when they may need it more.

Who Stands to Benefit the Most?

- People who currently spend over $4,000 a year for health care.

- People who spend little on health care, but are looking for additional retirement savings vehicles.

- People with extremely low income. Contributing to an HSA may lower their taxable income enough to help them qualify for the Earned Income Tax Credit, thereby substantially reducing their overall tax burden.

- People with an income around $56,000 per year. Again, contributing to an HSA may nudge them into a lower tax bracket, so they not only avoid taxes on their contributions, but pay less in taxes on their income.

- Small-business entrepreneurs and the self-employed, for whom health care costs have recently reached astronomical highs. HSAs can help these people make health care affordable again.

Lower Health Care Costs for Individuals and Business Owners

HSAs don't replace a normal or typical health insurance policy. They are designed as a supplement to a health insurance policy. If you're looking for the "catch," here it is: HSAs can only be set up if you've already got a high-deductible health insurance coverage policy.

Why? The short answer is that the pilot programs, including Archer Medical Savings Accounts, also known as MSAs (see below), were found to offer the greatest benefits per dollar when teamed with high-deductible plans. Studies also showed that people who were already comfortable with high-deductible health insurance policies found it easier to adapt to "self-managed" health care spending.

People with high deductibles were already paying out of their own pockets for doctors and care; most had already developed the skills to make the most of "pay-as-you-go" medicine.

The premium payments for high-deductible plans can be substantially less than half the price of full-coverage health insurance. So it's no surprise that young, single, and relatively healthy workers prefer high-deductible plans, whether the money for premiums comes out of their pocket (for the self-employed) or is taken out of a paycheck (through a high-deductible plan offered as a job benefit by an employer). Employers whose worker base is primarily young and single people have probably noticed that, when given a choice, most of these employees will choose a high-deductible plan. Often, these individuals may already be covered by a spouse's or parent's policy, and may even opt not to participate in their employer's health care plan.

Under the HSA program, deductibles are quite high:

- Individuals must have an annual deductible of at least $1,000.
- Families must have an annual deductible of at least $2,000.

High-deductible plans are sometimes called "hit-by-a-truck-insurance." Good plans pay for both catastrophic and routine medical care, once the insured person has paid out-of-pocket for the first $500 or $1,000 worth of medical fees. If you're healthy, this is a good gamble. Even in New York City, where the average cost of a doctor's office visit is $350, any person needing more than three doctor office visits per year can rest easy knowing that additional or more costly care — from doctors, specialists, or hospitals — will be paid for by the insurance plan. And in the unlikely event that the insured person does get hit by a truck, or needs that trip to the emergency room ($1,500 average in Manhattan), a few days' hospitalization ($600 per day), or surgery (thousands of dollars), a good high-deductible plan will cover all costs. Even the least expensive plans pay as much as 80 percent of all costs, once the deductible has been reached.

> - Annual out-of-pocket expenses for individuals must not exceed $5,100.*
> - Annual out-of-pocket expenses for families must not exceed $10,200.*
> *Amount listed is for 2005, indexed annually.

Not every high-deductible health plan qualifies (see Chapter 3, "Picking the Right High-Deductible Health Plan," for details). Another stipulation is that the plan must have what is considered a reasonable cap on out-of-pocket expenses:

An out-of-pocket maximum is the cumulative total a covered person will pay for medical care in any given year. If you reach this maximum, the insurance policy pays all remaining expenses. Depending on the health plan, some expenses — such as premiums or expenses for care received outside a provider network — may not count toward the out-of-pocket maximum. See your plan summary for details.

> A High-Deductible Plan Is REQUIRED for an HSA.
>
> - Individuals and families covered under traditional, full-coverage insurance plans (including Health Maintenance Organizations, Preferred Provider Options, Point-of-Service plans, Medicare and Medicaid) that do not meet the deductible minimum are not eligible for HSAs.
> - Individuals and families covered under traditional insurance can take advantage of the annual "benefit enrollment period" to explore whether switching to a higher-deductible coverage plan would be a good idea. If you're covered under an employer-provided plan, your employer will give you information about your options. Take advantage of it!

An executive with a $130,000 salary might easily afford to spend up to $10,000 for family care that isn't covered by his or her high-deductible family insurance plan. But a self-employed person, entry-level or low-wage worker making less than $23,000 per year might find it difficult to come up with an extra $5,000 to pay a year's worth of medical fees on a plan with a $5,000 family deductible. For many families earning wages and salaries above this lower level, HSAs represent a breakthrough strategy that can lower health care costs today and increase retirement savings for future health care needs.

In the best plans, and with the best strategy, people will choose the deductible limit that they are most comfortable with, within a range that stretches from $1,000 (for singles) to $10,000 (for a family).

Not everyone likes a high-deductible plan. People who get sick a lot, or have a history of needing more than routine preventive care in the course of a year, often choose to pay higher health insurance premiums in exchange for having their proportionately higher medical bills paid for by a broader coverage plan with lower deductibles.

And, not surprisingly, people who have children or other dependents (such as a disabled or unemployed spouse, frail elderly parent or other relative) usually opt for the peace of mind that a broader health care plan can give. Small businesses made up of family members, or companies whose workers tend to be mostly people with family responsibilities usually find that, when offered a choice, these workers resist switching from their existing full-service health plans created as HMOs or those with a PPO.

Health Care Premium Costs

That's not to say people haven't grumbled about how HMOs and PPOs perform as a worker benefit in light of their cost, or about how many of these plans restrict their choice of doctors and care options. To protect their families against unforeseen health care emergencies, fully insured workers have for many decades swallowed an increased share of premium costs — in some cases, painfully large sums are deducted from their weekly paychecks. In 2003 one survey of 5,300 small businesses, at those companies providing comprehensive medical insurance, the cost of medical programs represented 29% of the salaries on average. This expense was divided about equally between employer and employee.

Employers also pay more for each full-coverage health care policy, usually about two-thirds more than they will pay for each high-deductible policy. In many industries, having an "attractive benefits package" does indeed attract higher-quality workers. For some employers, it's well worth it to pay $600 per month - or as much as $1,500 per month for family coverage - to retain a happy and productive worker.

Unfortunately, not every company can afford to spend $600 per month on even their star employee. Smaller companies suffer the worst. An estimated 47 percent of American small businesses don't offer any sort of health insurance plan as a benefit — simply because they feel they can't afford it. If you work at one of these companies, an HSA could make a real difference in the way you pay for health care.

From the Databank: The Crushing Cost of Worker Health Care

The U.S. Federal Reserve's surveys of employers and other surveys find health costs to be a frequently mentioned worry among executives.

A random survey of 2,800 employers conducted last year found that the typical employer spent about $6,619 a year per family on health-insurance premiums; the typical employee paid an additional $2,412. Despite shifting costs to workers, employers' premiums have risen 38% during the past three years. In the past year, the U.S. government says employers' health costs have risen 10.5% while wages are up only 3%.

Source: *The Wall Street Journal*, March 11, 2004

The U.S. Government has looked at the results of this trend with dread; according to U.S. Department of Labor statistics, 85 percent of the 45 million uninsured are in working families, and 60 percent of the working uninsured are small-business employees (and their dependents). Today, many American families are entirely uninsured, with no health care coverage and, for many, no way to pay for an unexpected illness or emergency medical treatment. How to provide cost-effective good-quality health care to Americans, when they need it, has been a congressional concern and a political issue for more than a century.

Profile: Renée

Renée, 32, is a single mom. Her son Reese is fearless and accident-prone — he's broken three bones already, at age seven. She gets some child support from Reese's father, but not much.

Renée's mother recently moved in with them after fracturing a hip and losing much of her mobility. (Last year Renée spent several thousand dollars on airfare — and all her vacation time — traveling back and forth between her mother's house and her own home. She and her mother are both fiercely independent, but they've reluctantly conceded that living together may be the best arrangement for them.)

Having her mother in the house means that Renée's babysitting expenses have gone down, but just about every other expense has gone up — way up. She's had to renovate the bathroom with assist bars in the shower and by the toilet. There are three mouths to feed and more errands to run.

Renée's mother, so far, has been able to pay for her own health care. That's good, since she's still taking Celebrex for her hip, and the prescription costs hundreds of dollars. But Renée wants to be prepared for other medical crises, should they arrive. Between her mother and Reese, they probably will.

Renée works at a 25-person accounting firm. This year, the company is offering high-deductible health plans and HSAs. Renée has always been covered under the HMO, but she finds the new plan intriguing. For one thing, it won't restrict her to a narrow network of doctors. For another, it will let her pay for occasional massage therapy tax-free. Her premiums will be much lower, and — if she can manage not to spend the whole account every year — she'll have some retirement savings to complement her IRA.

Renée looks at her medical expenses from last year ($10,200 including premiums) and figures out how much they would have cost under the combination of high-deductible plan and HSA, ($7,400) factoring in the cost of premiums throughout the year. The number is actually lower under the high-deductible plan. Ever the accountant, Renee firmly believes that the numbers never lie. She signs up for the new plan. Naturally, these figures will vary with each situation but are based on an actual case.

Tax Relief for Individuals

The advent of HSAs won't single-handedly solve all the cost problems of U.S. health care. Our current skyrocketing costs are the result of decades of complicated policies and market forces. No single regulation will magically bring prices down and cover all the uninsured. But even though HSAs don't change the actual price of coverage, they can help you spend less to purchase it. Here's how.

In some ways, HSAs are similar to Keogh or 401(k) retirement accounts. Both employees and employers can fund contributions to an HSA savings account, and both can enjoy some tax advantages.

As with IRAs, Keoghs and 401(k) accounts, the money can be invested to gain interest or dividends. It can be channeled into stock or bond instruments, and any gains can accumulate tax-free and tax-deferred until retirement, death, or disability.

For the first year of the program, the amounts of money that you can invest through an HSA are relatively small and manageable. There are caps on the maximum amount of money that you can put into an HSA each year.

For individuals, the maximum amount of money that can be deposited into an HSA account this tax year 2005 is $2,650. If the account has been set up for a family (two or more people), the maximum that can be deposited is $5,250. The actual amounts allowable for contributions that qualify as a tax deduction depend on a few factors, such as the deductible on your health insurance plan. People who are over 55 but not yet retired are allowed to contribute additional money each calendar year ($600 in 2005 and increasing $100 per year up to $1,000 in 2009 and thereafter) to allow their savings to "catch up" before they reach the age of 65.

An "Above the Line" Tax Write-Off

Under this program, you don't have to itemize your HSA contributions to get the tax write-off for medical expenses. It comes right off the top — above the line — and gets deducted from your gross income. This is one reason why many tax accountants consider HSAs fairer to taxpayers: previously, only taxpayers who itemized their deductions could get a tax break on their medical spending.

Employer contributions to your HSA:
- Are excludable from your gross income, and not subject to withholding from wages or income tax
- Are not subject to taxes mandated by FICA, FUTA, or the Railroad Retirement Act.

When you contribute to an HSA:

- Your contributions are excludable from your gross income, and from income tax.
- Money saved in HSA accounts accumulates interest that is tax-deferred while it remains within the account.
- Money paid out from HSAs is not subject to any tax, as long as you use the money for qualified medical expenses. (If you withdraw the money for non-qualified expenses prior to age 65, it becomes taxable in that year and a tax penalty of 10% of the amount will apply.)

When an employer provides an HSA, the employer and the employee can both make contributions to the employee's HSA during the same tax year. Each gets a tax saving on the amount they each contribute. If your employer offers an HSA contribution, you could be throwing money away by not taking advantage of it. The Contribution Calculator in Chapter 5 can help determine how much employees and employers can deposit per year and still get the maximum amount of tax savings.

Tax deductible, tax-deferred, and tax-free: these are the advantages of using an HSA for a "second" retirement account. That is, HSAs aren't designed to be your primary retirement savings vehicle. Use a 401(k), SEP, IRA, or Keogh plan to provide for your retirement income. But use an HSA to give your retirement income a hefty supplement.

After you reach age 65, you can use your accumulated HSA funds (which can include interest or dividends from stock funds, bonds, or other high-yield instruments) for other things besides health care. After retirement, money you withdraw and use for non-qualifying expenses is taxed at the normal rate for investment income. However, money you use for qualifying expenses later in life — such as nursing home costs — can still be withdrawn with no tax paid. It is entirely tax-free.

How much can this "better rainy-day fund" contribute to your retirement years? One financial planner has estimated that someone saving $2,000 per year for 25 years at a five percent rate of return, the account would wind up worth several hundred thousand dollars. See page 96 for more details.

That's a best-case scenario. Perhaps, most people will wind up spending more HSA money than they can save. Interest rates and return on investments might not be as good as ten percent per year. But some money will be saved. That's better than the worst-case scenario — the one where you end up old, unable to work and with nothing left in the bank.

The HSA Advantage:

- Tax savings
- Ownership
- Portability
- Control
- Freedom

Other advantages of an HSA, besides tax savings, include ownership and portability, and the control and flexibility of consumer-directed health care.

You own your HSA. If you leave your current employer, you can take the money with you. If you're self-employed, an HSA can offer relief to two pressing problems: affordable health care and high self-employment taxes.

WILL HSAs WORK FOR YOU? TAKE THE "DEMOGRAPHICS TEST"

This simple test can help you decide no matter how many employees you have, or if you only have one (self-employed).

1. For each full-time employee (include yourself) score 1 point.

2. For each employee between ages 21-30, score 10 points.

3. For each employee already participating in an IRA, Keogh or 401(k) plan, score 10 points.

4. For each employee with gross income over $50,000, score 10 points.

5. For each employee already covered by another's health plan (spouse or parent) deduct 5 points.

6. For each full-time worker with a gross income under $23,000, deduct 1 point.

TOTAL

RESULTS: If your total is over 20 points, your business can benefit from participating in the HSA program. If your score is higher than 100 points, your business may reduce health care costs by a significant margin with an HSA strategy in place this tax year.

If your score is lower than 20 points, you may not have the necessary cash flow or capital to get the best benefit from the HSA program. If this is the case, meeting with a tax advisor this tax year may provide some direction for achieving this goal in future years.

Figure 1-1

You can use the HSA to pay for any qualified medical expense (including health insurance deductibles and out-of-pocket payments for medical services, products, and prescriptions), as defined by the IRS. Because HSAs are not insurance policies, they don't impose restrictions such as preauthorization of services, and you always have your choice of doctors. HSAs are meant to encourage participants to become better health care consumers. When every dollar you spend on health care could be earning interest in your account, you'll think more about your medical decisions.

There is a short worksheet on page 51 to test whether an HSA is a good fit for you.

Evolution of an Idea: HSAs, MSAs, HRAs, FSPs and FSAs

Health Savings Accounts (HSAs) represent the latest evolution of U.S. policy programs to improve worker health care. Much of the groundwork was laid during the pilot programs for Medical Savings Accounts (1996–2003). While this federal program was largely superceded in 2004 by the creation of HSAs, MSAs can still be set-up through December 31, 2005.

Keeping the Abbreviations Straight

The "A" always stands for "account," but unfortunately that doesn't help much. This section should give you a better idea of the options that may be available to you.
- HRA: Health Reimbursement Account
- FSA: Flexible Spending Account (you may also see these referred to by the category of the expenses they cover—as in Health Care Spending Accounts or Dependent Care Spending Accounts, for example)
- FSP: Flexible Spending Plan, structured much like an FSA
- MSA: Medical Savings Account (also known as an Archer MSA)

The insurance industry, in cooperation with IRS mandates, has also made a few different kinds of "medical savings plans" available as a health benefit for employees of large corporations, although with fairly mixed results. Some of these plans are still operating, though most employees will likely find them inferior to HSAs.

Health Reimbursement Accounts (HRAs) began life as a perk for the executive suite. The IRS approves these certain plans, which allow for cash compensation to well-paid employees that does not have to be included as "wages." Ostensibly, the money goes to reimburse medical expenses not covered by the company insurance policy plan, and the company can take the amounts as a business tax deduction.

HRAs in Brief

HRAs are provided by employers. You can't start one on your own. An HRA might amass money over time, but you might not be allowed to take any of that money with you if you leave your job before retirement.

When HRAs were extended to rank-and-file workers, the corporate tax benefits remained, but employees were given stricter guidelines about what medical expenses could be reimbursed. The employer funds HRAs entirely, gets a tax write-off for the amount, and reimbursements to the employee are not counted as part of the employees' gross income.

HRA dollars are set-asides, essentially virtual accounts that are funded only when claims are filed. Workers pay their own medical bills, and then get reimbursed by the employer if the expense meets the guidelines.

Money in an HRA can be spent *only* on qualifying medical expenses. Emergency withdrawals are not permitted.

The downside for employers is that the business funds these accounts. The downside to employees, with HRAs, is that the business, not the employee, controls the money. If workers don't ask for reimbursement, the business doesn't have to spend an extra dime beyond administrative costs.

A Comparison of Employee Benefit Plans

	HSAs	HRAs	FSAs/FSPs
Who Is Eligible?	Employees Retirees Owners	Employees Retirees Owners	Employees
What is Maximum Yearly Contribution?*	$2,650-$5,250	No Maximum	No Maximum
Who Controls and Owns the Account?	Employee	Employer	Employer
How is the Money Disbursed?	Checks or Debit Card	Reimburse through Employer	Check, Debits, Withdrawal slips
Who Contributes to The Account?	Employers or Employees	Employer Only	Employee Only
Is it Portable?	Yes	No	No
Can the Money Earn Interest or Dividends?	Yes	No	No
Can the Money be Used for Non-health Emergency Spending?	Yes	No	Some (Section 125 Rules)
Can the Money "Roll Over" to Accumulate?	Yes	No	No
What Are the Tax Advantages?	Tax Free to Employee; Deductible To Business	Tax Free to Employee; Deductible To Business	Tax Free to Employee Only
Is High-Deductible Insurance Required?	Yes	No	No

*Amount listed is for 2005, indexed annually.

Figure 1-2

Just in Case All These Names Weren't Confusing Enough . . .

When HRA plans were first introduced, some employers—to emphasize saving over spending—referred to them as "Health Savings Accounts." Fortunately, now that "Health Savings Account" has a specific legal meaning, these plan names will probably be changed to reflect the account structure more accurately. If your employer currently offers something called a Health Savings Account, look closely at how it works. If you can't contribute to the account or take it with you when you leave the company, it's really an HRA in disguise.

In contrast, Flexible Spending Accounts (FSAs) and Flexible Spending Plans (FSPs) are funded only by the employee, through agreed-upon payroll deductions, and deposited to a special account administered by the employer. These amounts are tax-advantaged to both employers and employees, because they are "top of the line" deductions, not subject to Social Security, Medicare, state or federal income tax. In this way they are similar to HSAs.

Typically, Flexible plans can be used to pay for health expenses not covered by an employer health plan, such as out-of-network providers or prescription medicines not covered by the policy. Employees can access their money directly, through a debit card or by writing a check.

The Bare-Bones Guide

Right now, your employer may give you access to as many as three different kinds of health-related accounts. Here's how to keep them straight:

HRA: It's your employer's money. You can spend it, but you probably can't keep it.
FSA: It's *your* money. You can spend it, but you can't keep it. In fact, if you don't spend it, your employer gets to keep it.
HSA: It's your money, and sometimes your employer's money as well. You can always spend it or keep it—or both.

FSAs and FSPs can also be used to pay for dependent care, such babysitting, day care, or companions or adult day health programs for an older family member, if the employer decides these expenses can qualify. (These expenses, however, cannot be reimbursed by the same account that reimburses medical expenses. You must set up a separate account, often called a Dependent Care FSA, to save and pay for these costs. The inflexibility of these account structures can be frustrating for many.)

Like HRAs, the downside of FSAs is that they are locked within an account that is monitored and administered by the employer — even though the employee's money funds the plan. And, under current law, there is no "rollover." If an employee does not use up the entire amount by the end of the benefit year, the money not used goes to the employer. The employee forfeits the balance. It is a "use it or lose it" benefit.

The worse downside is that an employee who quits or gets fired no longer has access to the money in the account. This forfeit is particularly galling, since it's the worker's money, not the employer's, that funds the account. Under some account structures, you may still request reimbursement for expenses you incurred before you left your job.

Some accounts, under COBRA, do let you continue participating through the end of the year, even if you're no longer an employee. But in most circumstances, you cannot be reimbursed for expenses you incur after your employment ends, which means you're back in the same situation—forfeiting your money to your former employer.

COBRA stands for Consolidated Omnibus Budget Reconciliation Act; it refers to a law that helps employees hang on to their health coverage when their employment ends. For more about COBRA, see Chapter 6.

The "use it or lose it" aspect of FSPs and FSAs does nothing to curb health care spending. Typically, employees with FSAs schedule extra medical appointments for late in the year, treat themselves to several pairs of new eyeglasses or a round of therapeutic massages — anything to spend down the balance before it is lost.

---

as

the People

), your HSA dollars are "portable" — you can open HSAs with or without employer involvement.
- Dollars put into accounts are owned by the employee and not subject to vesting requirements or "use it or lose it" rules.
- Dollars put into accounts are tax-free for both employer and employee.
- HSAs are inheritable assets; they can be passed on to a spouse or heir if the account holder dies.

As of this writing, Senator Charles Grassley (R—IA) had asked the U.S. Treasury to consider doing away with the use-it-or-lose-it rule. If that rule is removed, you will—in theory—be able to carry forward balances in your FSA from year to year. So if you have an employer-sponsored FSA, you'll want to pay close attention to any updates from your employer about changes in plan structure or regulation.

HRAs remain a practical solution for companies with low-wage workers. In the most generous plans, employers commit to reimburse for an amount equal to the worker's deductible limit.

While all their health care expenses are ultimately covered, employees have an incentive to keep their medical costs low: they have to use their own money first, and get reimbursed later. In fact, HRAs can be used in tandem with HSAs, to help low-wage workers meet some medical costs not covered by their high-deductible insurance policy plans (See Chapter 9, "The HRA Three-Step.")

Why Flexible Spending Plans Are Finished

Because Flexible Spending Plans have so many strings attached, it's hard to imagine that any worker would choose an FSA, if offered an HSA. While some insurance experts are still trying to make the case for flexible spending, the IRS has been further defining HSAs to make FSAs obsolete. A recent ruling for "transitional relief" will allow people to qualify for an HSA if their employer-sponsored health plans offer an FSA in the form of a prescription drug card, provided that expenses for prescriptions are subject to the deductible limits of the plan.

The "use it or lose it" aspects of FSAs don't encourage workers to spend their health care dollars wisely.   One solution proposed by the National Association of Health Underwriters would be to change the FSA laws to allow leftover funds to be rolled over, or allow the remaining funds to be switched into HSAs. At least one senator (see sidebar on page 36) agrees.

On May 12, 2004, the U.S. Congress passed HR 4279, a bill that would allow individuals to roll over up to $500 of unused FSA money into the following year, or into a new HSA. At this writing the change awaits Senate approval: under current law, transferring funds from HRAs or FSAs to HSAs is not allowed.

An Advantage for Early Movers (those who act ahead of others)

The HSA concept was designed specifically to benefit small businesses, from sole proprietorships to family LLCs (limited liability corporations) and up to the small corporate enterprise. Large corporations can also initiate HSA programs, but small business owners and the self-employed can initiate them faster, and should get the most benefits in the current tax year. Individuals and companies who haven't been able to afford health insurance can use the HSA program to help them get inexpensive yet comprehensive coverage for their health care needs. And—as we saw on page 96—the sooner you start building your savings, the more they can grow.

For the many people who are working full-time for someone else, yet have a small independent business on the side, dollars put into an HSA program can be the "better rainy-day fund." It can be a second retirement savings account, one that serves as an additional tax deduction — a tax shelter — for the income generated from that small, part-time business.

People who have been afraid to leave the comfort of a corporate job because of its health care benefits now have a new incentive to join entrepreneurial businesses — or may even start their own — without having to sacrifice good-quality health care for their families.

Portability is an early-mover advantage for people who are self-employed, or for those for whom owning their own business has been a lifelong dream. Most certainly, the program will change and evolve even as these early movers help to shape its final form. While the program was a bipartisan effort by members of the U.S. Congress, as part of the Medicare Reform Act of 2003, it's sure to be tinkered with.

This book has been prepared by using the Guidelines published by the IRS for the HSA program in 2004. Readers should expect the IRS to also weigh in on changes to the program. Under the new law, the IRS has been given the power to adjust contribution levels, tax account-ability, reporting practices, and exactly which medical services qualify to be covered and may be paid for tax-free. Adjustments for inflation are already in the mix—meaning your maximum permissible contri-bution and out-of-pocket expenses will likely increase in future years.

The federal government estimates that between three and five million Americans will take advantage of this new program in its first year. Should you be among them? Can you be? Turn to the next chapter and find out.

How MSAs Integrate with HSAs

The Working Families Tax Relief Act of 2004 (P.L. 108-311) extends the Archer MSA program by allowing taxpayers to establish new accounts through December 31, 2005.

According to IRS Notice 2004-2, the pertinent part:

Q-12. How much may be contributed to an HSA in calendar year 2004?

A-12. The maximum annual contribution to an HSA is the sum of the limits determined separately for each month, based on status, eligibil-ity and health plan coverage as of the first day of the month.

All HSA contributions made by or on behalf of an eligible individual to an HSA are aggregated for purposes of applying the limit. The annual limit is decreased by the aggregate contributions to an Archer MSA.

HSAs: THE BASICS

HSAs are "the better rainy-day fund" approach to health care.

HSAs can only be used in combination with a high-deductible health insurance policy.

HSA contributions are from pre-tax dollars, which can be made by the company and/or the individual.

HSAs are portable benefits, controlled and owned by individuals.

HSAs can "roll over" from year to year as accumulated tax-free savings.

HSA payouts for qualified medical expenses are tax-free.

HSAs interest and dividends are tax-free until retirement.

HSAs are expected to encourage participants to become better health care consumers.

Eligibility Requirements And Your Financial Plans

2

While the scope of the HSA program is broad, the eligibility requirements are new, complex and innovative. Although not everyone who wants an HSA can get one, HSAs are open to a wide range of groups of employers and employees.

Who Qualifies?

Any individual with a qualifying high-deductible health plan who:
- Is not claimed as a dependent by anyone else
- Is not entitled to or enrolled in benefits under Medicare
- Has no other health coverage

What Types of Businesses Qualify?

Any business — a sole proprietorship, limited liability partnership (LLP), corporation or nonprofit corporation — may implement an HSA plan.

A Business Needs How Many Employees to Qualify?

Only one — yourself — if you are self-employed. HSAs impose no restrictions on the number of employees involved; they are available to the single self-employed individual as well as to the employee of a multinational corporation.

How Do Individuals or Individual Workers Become Eligible for an HSA?

An eligible individual can set up an HSA with or without the involvement of his or her employer. Anyone is eligible who meets the following requirements:

1. They have a qualifying high-deductible health insurance policy in force before the date they open their HSA account.
2. They are not receiving benefits under Medicare Part A or Part B.
3. They are not claimed as a dependent on another person's tax return.
4. They are not covered by any other type of health insurance plan that is not a high-deductible plan.

This last is the definitive issue with the HSA program. If you are already covered by a full-benefits health plan (also known as a "first dollar" coverage plan, with no copays), you may see no reason to switch to a high-deductible plan. But if you don't have a qualifying high-deductible plan, you are not eligible to open an HSA.

Yet for the employee with little or no health care expense, an HSA could mean as much as $2,650 in individual savings or $5,250 in family savings for 2005, (indexed annually) and provided in part by an employer. Of course, you may need to spend some funds for health care costs, but the unspent portion of the nest egg can grow with investment dividends.

Healthy and Wealthy

An HSA can help you make medical expenses more affordable. But if you have few medical expenses, your HSA could be a potent savings vehicle — allowing you to set aside several thousand dollars each year.

Example: The Design Team

Barbara, Bernice and Cathy decide to open a small, part-time interior-design business together. Barbara has been unemployed for a while and is currently uninsured. Bernice recently lost her job in a furniture showroom and is on COBRA, which she is finding quite expensive. Cathy still works full-time (she will work on the new venture on weekends) and has an HMO insurance plan through her corporate employer.

Barbara and Bernice want to get a small group policy to get cheaper insurance. However, Cathy doesn't see a need to join this group plan. She likes her HMO.

Barbara and Bernice each get a high-deductible ($2,500) policy that will qualify them to open HSAs. The monthly premiums for the plan are relatively low, costing Bernice hundreds of dollars less than she was paying to continue her COBRA coverage. Cathy does not have a qualifying plan, and as long as she sticks with her HMO, she cannot open an HSA at this time.

Later, if Cathy's employer makes a high-deductible plan available in her next enrollment period, one that qualifies its participants to start HSAs, Cathy might decide to switch from her HMO to this high-deductible policy. Instead of starting a new group plan with Barbara and Bernice, she can stay with this insurance, which is partially paid for by her corporate employer. But now she can open her own HSA to shelter the income she makes working with Barbara and Bernice on their joint venture.

Cathy does not need to have her current full-time employer involved in the HSA account. Her employer and her employer's insurer do not need to know about her second job or about the HSA.

Other Allowable Insurance Plans

The law does allow people already covered under certain kinds of other health care insurance to open an HSA account. These are called "permitted insurance" in the law. The other kinds of insurance you can have in addition to a high-deductible health insurance policy are:
- Separate dental and/or vision care insurance, or flexible spending accounts (FSAs) covering only dental and/or vision care
- Discount cards for health care services or products (for example, prescription drugs)
- Disease management and wellness programs, as long as they do not "provide significant benefits in the nature of medical care"
- Employee assistance plans, again if they do not "provide significant benefits" (short-term counseling is okay)
- FSAs or HRAs that pay or reimburse for medical expenses after a high deductible has been met*
- Separate long-term care insurance
- Worker's compensation insurance (through employers)
- Disability insurance (individual or through unions or employment)
- Automobile insurance (including coverage for medical care in accidents and emergencies)

- Business liability insurance
- Insurance that pays for fixed amount of hospitalization
- Freestanding health insurance for travel (such as flight insurance or automatic travel coverage when transport is booked on a credit card)

Note: IRS Rev. Rule 2004-45 clarified that employers may offer HRAs or FSAs that pay or reimburse additional fees for coinsurance or out-of-pocket costs, provided that the individual has already satisfied his or her in-network deductible on the policy. Retirement HRAs funded by employers — accounts that will only pay for or reimburse medical expenses incurred after retirement — are permitted for individuals making contributions to their HSAs while they are still employed. For more on coinsurance, see Chapter 3, and "The HRA Three-Step" in Chapter 9.

Who Will Not Qualify?

HSAs are not available to persons who are both eligible for and enrolled in Medicare. Most Americans qualify for Medicare at age 65; however, if an individual continues to work past that age, remains enrolled in a high-deductible health plan, and does not apply for Medicare benefits, he or she may qualify to contribute to an HSA.

People over the age of 55 have some extra incentives to get into the program. They can contribute up to $600 more this 2005 to their HSA accounts, and even more in future years, to help them "catch up" to younger investors and grow their new nest egg before they reach retirement age.

If you're claimed as a dependent on someone else's tax forms — regardless of whether that someone is a spouse, a domestic partner, or a parent — you cannot open your own HSA.

Children not of working age cannot open their own HSAs with money given by their parents. Children who work but are claimed as dependents on their parents' tax return cannot open their own HSAs. In this respect, HSAs are different from other forms of trusts and savings accounts parents may create on behalf of their children.

Similarly, a non-working spouse or any other relative who is claimed as a dependent on another person's tax return cannot open his or her own HSA either.

These dependents will still benefit from the medical coverage provided through a family high-deductible health insurance policy. The money put into an HSA that has been tied to a family policy can still be taken out for family members when they have medical needs. The tax-paying breadwinner still gets the tax breaks for HSA contributions — but no one else in the family may make these tax-free contributions.

This has relevance to the question of whether or not family members who work in a family business should be considered employees for tax purposes. See Chapter 7.

HSAs AS PART OF YOUR EMPLOYEE HEALTH BENEFITS PACKAGE

The patchwork of health insurance packages available today has created a confusing mix. Some workers have insurance; some business owners do not. Some people are covered under someone else's insurance policy — a wife, a husband, a child, an adoptee or domestic partner. Some health insurance policies are good — but only if you don't get sick! Some are generously comprehensive — but too expensive to pay for.

The Nondiscrimination Rules for HSAs

If an employer offers a high-deductible health insurance plan as part of a "cafeteria plan," or as an option among many types of plans, it must make the high-deductible plan available to ALL employees. And if the employer makes a yearly contribution to one worker's HSA account, the employer must also make an identical yearly contribution to all other workers who both have HSA accounts and have chosen the high-deductible insurance plan during that tax year.

The employer does not have to make a monetary contribution on behalf of employees who did not elect the high-deductible insurance policy plan.

Who Will Benefit the Most from HSAs?

Clearly, those who would prefer a high-deductible on their health insurance policy, or already have one, are poised to get the most benefit from this new program.

The First Ones on Board

- Workers in their 20s
- Single people with no dependents
- Individuals earning over $50,000 a year
- Those who already participate in an IRA or 401(k)
- Low-wage workers will probably be more reluctant, but they may
    stand to gain the most.

If you are self-employed, and don't have any insurance policy at all, a low-cost, high-deductible plan that qualifies for an HSA is a smart place to start.

If you work for someone else, you're likely to hear about HSAs in your workplace in the next few years. Odds are, the smaller your company, the sooner you'll hear about HSAs. Small businesses have been hit particularly hard by recent increases in health care costs, and many may be eager to avail themselves of the savings associated with HSAs.

Health care policy experts point to survey after survey indicating that small businesses and large corporations alike are increasingly concluding that employees must bear more of the costs for their health insurance. For employees, HSAs offer the best opportunity to build a retirement stake within the framework of an inevitable trend.

Self-Employed? Small Business?

The smaller the company, the faster its employees can benefit from HSAs. And even if you work for a larger company, you don't have to wait for your employer to adopt HSAs — you can still purchase your own high-deductible coverage and open an HSA on your own.

But let's cut to the chase, and punt to the pundits: some of the best minds in the insurance and tax industry have pored over the possibilities of the HSA program. Their research seems to suggest that those who can get the most out of it share certain characteristics.

Generally, workers who are young adults (over 21 but under age 30) will go for the program.

Predominantly single workers, responsible only for their own insurance needs (i.e., with no children or other dependent to support), will go for the program.

Highly paid workers (over $50,000) will go for the program on the strength of its tax-advantaged possibilities.

If you rely on a relative for health insurance coverage, you're probably less enthusiastic about HSAs. In fact, workers getting health insurance through a spouse or parent are the least likely to apply for insurance through their workplace, although some may consider switching if financial incentives (such as employer contributions to an HSA) are offered to them.

Low-wage workers (earning under $23,000) will have very little enthusiasm for HSAs. These employees may find it hard to set aside anything for savings, especially if they have family to support. However, if you're in this income bracket, you're young, you have an entry-level job, and you anticipate a career with salary growth, you may go for the program on the strength of its portability and its potential as a retirement savings tool. Those who already participate in an IRA or 401(k) will very likely embrace this program, too.

A Quick Quiz for Self-Employed Individuals

Quick — how much did you spend on your vacation travels last year?

Did you spend $5,000? $3,000? Or less than $1,000?

With HSAs, you will need to have money at hand to meet all medical expenses until you reach your deductible limit. Vacation spending can be a good indicator of discretionary income and your ability to save: if you were able to afford a $5,000 vacation last year, you should be able to afford a $5,000 deductible policy. Conversely, if you kept vacation expenses under $1,000, you may experience difficulty meeting a deductible higher than $1,000.

How Much Will It Cost?

The next step in determining if HSAs are right for you is to calculate exactly what health care coverage costs you today. Reducing that cost on a monthly or yearly schedule will be your goal.

Myth: "I Can't Afford Health Insurance!"

The monthly premium costs for high-deductible health insurance (the only kind that qualifies for the HSA program) are generally only a third of the cost of premiums for a typical, full-coverage HMO. The monthly premium can be less than a $100 per person in a good group plan. Chapter 3 offers some suggestions on finding and joining a group plan even if you're self-employed.

Focus for a bit on how the amount you pay as premium costs for health insurance can serve as a business tax deduction. **If you're self-employed,** you are entitled to write off the entire cost of your self-insured health insurance premiums as an above-the-line deduction on your personal income taxes.

But **if you run a business with just your spouse,** you can "hire" the spouse as your employee, and write off your "employee's" insurance premiums as a business deduction. (If you buy your spouse a high-deductible family policy, you'll be covered as well — for one inclusive price.)

If your business is incorporated, and you pay yourself a salary, you can write off the entire cost of your premiums, and the premiums for any employees, as a business deduction.

If you're an employee at someone else's corporation and you receive employer-sponsored health care, your portion of premiums is deducted from your pay before tax. You've already got those savings. But you may have seen the amount of the premium get higher and higher in recent years. By switching to an combination of high-deductible plan and HSA, you may be able to reduce the amount and still get the tax advantage.

Calculating Costs and Savings For The Self-Employed

If you're self-employed, and you don't have any insurance coverage, you know what your current health insurance costs are. They're zero. You're not paying anything in health insurance policy premiums. (As long as you don't ever, ever, get sick or hurt, this will work for you. However, your luck can't hold forever. A Small Business Digest survey of self-employed individuals indicated sickness was the most feared catastrophe for 71% of the 680 respondents.)

And what are your actual medical care costs? Most successful self-employed people keep good personal records, and odds are good you've got a folder or file or a shoebox marked "medical receipts." Looking through these records will give you some idea of what your out-of-pocket expenses were for the year; you may not have been able to deduct any of these if you did not itemize deductions on the Schedule A.

I Knew I Kept That for a Reason!

As you evaluate your health care spending, don't just look at insurance forms and explanations of benefits. Examine:
- Last year's tax returns
- Receipts
- Medical records
- Old checkbook registers
- Credit card statements
Remember that the IRS has a broader definition of health care expenses than most insurance plans do. See Chapter Six for details.

If you did pay for health insurance premiums, pull out last year's tax return and see what you deducted for self-employed health insurance (Line 31 on Form 1040 in 2004).

If you weren't actively self-employed last year, check your last year's tax return for itemized deductions for medical expenses (which would mean the amount exceeded 7.5 percent of your adjusted gross income!) on Form 1040's Schedule A. If your employer paid for only part of your health insurance premiums, the amount your boss took out of your paycheck for your share of the premiums will be listed as on your W-2 form for the last tax year. (Yes, even though your boss bought your insurance, you paid something for the premium — and the privilege of being insured on someone else's dime.) Put that down on Worksheet #1 on page 51 on the premium cost line.

If you left or lost a job, and have been paying a COBRA for continuation of your health insurance coverage, put that down as a premium cost on your worksheet.

Now, go through your checkbook, and add up what you paid out-of-pocket for doctor bills, dentist care, and the like. Your credit card statements (especially the end-of-year summaries) will show you where

you paid for drugstore prescriptions and over-the-cou[n]
You should also think about whether last year you de[c]
new eyeglasses, or installed a treadmill at home on t[he]
doctor (these are just two items that may qualify as a .... ,
with an HSA plan).

You should now have two numbers on your worksheet. One number
is the amount of money you personally paid in health insurance coverage premiums, for you and for your family. It might be zero, if you
paid nothing for premiums. Or, it may be a hefty four-figure number,
if you've been paying for COBRA since you were last employed.

The other number is the amount you paid out-of-pocket for medical
care throughout the year, for yourself (and if applicable) for your
family.

We'll keep these numbers separate for a while.

Estimating Savings for the Self-Employed

Under the HSA program, you still have to consider two types of costs.

You still have to pay premiums to carry health insurance coverage.
Fortunately, in most states, the premiums for a high-deductible health
insurance plan can be roughly one-third of the cost of premiums for
other forms of health insurance.

Why is this? According to insurance underwriters, high-deductible
plans are generally more predictable. Insurance companies know how
much they can charge for a premium and still make a good profit, and
they are also smart enough to know that anyone shopping for a high-
deductible plan is going to be budget-minded. So, to stay competitive, insurance companies keep their high-deductible premiums quite
low.

Why Are High-Deductible Health Plans So Cheap?

- They're more predictable for insurance
- They attract healthy, budget-conscious consumers who are careful
    about how they use health care
- Many people with high-deductible coverage rarely reach their
    deductible — so the plans often don't have to pay benefits.
- The bottom line: High-deductible health plans are profitable for
    insurers. Of course, when you open an HSA, you profit too.

Medical Expenses are low for most of us. This chart shows Annual Medical Expenses for the United States population by percentage:

Money Spent on Medical Care Annually
Percentage of U.S. Population

No Medical Expenses $0	33%
$1 - $500	40%
$501 - $1,000	9%
$1,001 - $2,000	7%
$2,001 - $5,000	6%
$5,001 - $10,000	3%
$10,001 - $25,000	3%
$25,001 - $50,000	.5%
$50,001 - $100,000	.2%
$100,001 - And Up	.05%

Seventy-three percent of the population spend $500 or less on Medical Expenses per year. Most people will not spend all of their HSA funds in a year. What is not spent is yours to keep and earn interest.

Source: American Health Value   *Figure 2-1*

Rates vary considerably state by state, even for identical plans through the same provider. Here are some samples of what's available from providers at this writing:

If any of the above may apply to your situation, you might use these numbers. Or, you can leave this part until you've reviewed Chapter 3 and called a few providers. Then you could plug in some of those actual numbers for the premium fees.

The second type of estimated cost is how much you think you might pay out in out-of-pocket, pay-as-you-go health services over the next year.

You don't know if you or someone in your family will get sick. You may generally know if it's been too long between full dental checkups, with X-rays, or whether you need a mammogram, or want new eyeglasses in a modern style. (Last year's calendar or planner, if you have it, can jog your memory.) You can't guess if a bus will hit you.

There's one thing you can be sure of, under the HSA program, you'll probably never have to pay out-of-pocket any sum that looms larger than your deductible.

If you've chosen a $1,000 deductible, you probably won't have to pay out any more than $1,000. If you've chosen a $3,000 deductible for a family plan, the most you might pay out of your own pocket next year is $3,000.

Whatever your deductible is, add that figure to Worksheet #1.
Total up what you paid last year (A) and the maximum of what you might expect to pay next year (B).

Subtract (B) from (A). If the result (C) is less than (A), congratulations! You've just demonstrated how to save your dollars on health care, using the HSA program.

Total Estimated health care Expenses

Cost of premiums and out-of-pocket expenses in Previous Year (fees up to deductibles, co-pays, uncovered expenses, and medication)

Estimated Total for High-Deductible Insurance Premiums in New Year   TOTAL A ☐

Total of Deductible Under Insurance Policy in New Year
                                                                        TOTAL B ☐

Subtract "B" from "A" to get estimated cost savings for new plan, new year   TOTAL C ☐

Figure 2-2 WORKSHEET #1.

"But wait," you say. "My (C) is a bigger number than (A). I'll wind up paying more on this program!"

For some readers, this may be how the worksheet turns out. But remember, this is the worst-case scenario. It assumes you *are* going to get hit by a bus, or have other, highly serious medical needs in your family in the next year.

But odds are that you won't. And even if you do max out to your deductible, you'll be covered by the high-deductible policy, which has a low cost. In fact, because you are paying premiums with your own money, you'll probably pick the least expensive high-deductible premium plan that suits your needs. You'll also continue to be cautious with your health care spending: not running to the doctor for every sniffle, for example. The odds say you will spend something, but you will also manage to save.

Insurance actuaries know, from decades of statistics, that people who buy high-deductible health insurance policies very rarely spend up to the limit of their deductible in a calendar year. The majority doesn't even make it halfway. That's another reason why high-deductible plans are comparatively cheap — health insurance companies know they'll be seeing much more of your money than you will of theirs. They know you will be a penny-pincher where your own pennies are involved. The odds favor the house.

With the HSA program, the odds favor you. With managed care (the HMO, POS and PPO plans you're used to), if you don't spend a lot of your own money meeting a deductible, that's just good luck. With an HSA, you get to keep any money you put into the account and don't spend in a calendar year, and you may use it to pay towards your deductible in the *next* benefit year. Over time, the amounts not used accumulate within the account. Your "better rainy-day fund" can grow each year. If, five or ten years down the line, you really need the money for medical care. . . it's there for you. And it's been accumulating interest all the while.

Example: Janet

Janet's coworkers call her a hypochondriac, but she prefers to think of herself as thorough. On her hiking trip she had sniffles and sore knees. It turned out to be a case of allergies and ill-fitting boots, but it *could* have been Lyme disease. You never know. Janet doesn't take chances. She was at the doctor's office before they'd even unpacked the tent.

Janet works in the HR department — she works so hard she's been screened four times for carpal-tunnel syndrome — and she knows exactly how to get coverage under the company HMO. She uses it for all it's worth on each of three pre-existing conditions her screenings have turned up. But she still manages to spend a bundle on maintenance medications and occasional services the HMO won't cover (like her monthly acupuncture treatments).

So when the company (which employs about 200 people) announces it's moving to a consumerist approach, starting a new high-deductible health plan with an HSA, Janet is skeptical. "No way," she tells her husband. "We'd spend so much money on things we get for free under the HMO."

What Janet doesn't know is that an individual who spends more than $4,000 per year in out-of-network or uncovered expenses will typically wind up paying less with an HSA program.

The numbers bear this out. When Janet completes Worksheet #1, her amount A is $4,700. Her deductible under the new high-deductible plan, her amount B, is $2,000. Janet subtracts B from A and can't believe it: If next year's health care expenses are like this year's, she could save $2,700.

Example 2: Alan, Chris, and Judy

Alan, Chris and Judy — all 30 — have co-founded a nonprofit theater company. All actors, they've hung onto part-time "day jobs." But they'd really like to work in the theater full-time. Health insurance has proved so elusive — especially for Chris, whose jobs have included cutting hair and tending bar — that they joke they'll know they've hit the big time when they have medical coverage.

As for retirement savings, Judy has been fortunate: she's done enough film work to join the Screen Actors Guild, and she now qualifies for a small pension from that union. Alan has supported himself with office jobs, and he's managed to put a little money (though no means enough) in a 401(k). Chris, on the other hand, reaches his 30th birthday and starts to panic. He hasn't saved a penny for retirement — and though he can't imagine ever wanting to retire from theater, he doesn't want to still be working odd jobs at 70.

When Chris learns about HSAs, they seem like the solution to several problems at once. He takes a look at Worksheet #1. Amount A is low for him; he's in good shape and visits the doctor only once or twice a year, paying the entire price of the visit. He estimates he'll have $500 in health-related expenses next year. Amount B, his deductible, is

$1,500. Wait a second — could switching to a health savings account actually penalize him $1,000?

Not likely. Chris probably won't come within shouting distance of his deductible. In the past four years, he's needed emergency care only once — when he cut a finger while slicing limes at the bar — and his employer paid for it that time. Of course, he *could* be in a car accident, or he could live out the actor's nightmare and actually break a leg. But now he knows that if that ever happened, he wouldn't be stuck with more than $1,500 of the bill. He can afford that.

For Chris, the real payoff of the high-deductible plan/HSA combo is that he no longer has to worry about the kind of financial setback that could land him in a permanent day job. He can actually afford to follow his dreams.

Chris's enthusiasm for his new HSA gets Alan and Judy thinking about starting their own. They may be about to hit the big time after all.

Clearly, HSAs can benefit individuals who have few health care expenses. But HSAs will also benefit those who find themselves paying out-of-pocket for extensive medical care. For anyone now spending more than $4,000 per year, like Janet on page 52, the "C" on their worksheet may be substantially less than their "A," and they can save without any compromise on the quality of their health care.

Remember that plan rates vary not just by state, but by individual health history and how many family members will also be covered. Rather than try to provide general rates, let's compare some actual rates — for three individuals who work for an Ohio housewares company. They are:

Bob, 42, the married owner, who opted for the $10,000 family deductible for his wife, 42, son 18, and daughter, 13.
John, 56, the shop foreman, who opted for the $5,000 family deductible for his wife, 51, and two sons 18 and 19 years old.
Joan, 28, a single shop worker with no dependents, who took a $1,000 deductible individual plan.

All three previously had $250 deductibles, with $10 copays; maternity benefits were not included. Monthly premiums for each of them under this previous PPO plan were:

	Prior
Bob	$972 (Family)
John	$621 (Family)
Joan	$300 (Single)

New rates were provided as of June 1, 2004, from their insurer and are based on the relatively clean medical history of these three individuals.

Monthly premiums for each of them now are:

	Now	Prior
Bob	$331	$972 (Family)
John	$345	$621 (Family)
Joan	$101	$300 (Single)

As you can see, premiums are roughly one-third of what they were under the previous plan. Now, how will this work for your situation.

ELIGIBILITY: THE BASICS

You are eligible for an HSA account if:

- You are enrolled in a high-deductible health insurance policy that qualifies according to current IRS rules

- You are NOT entitled to Medicare benefits at this time

- You are NOT a dependent on anyone else's tax return

- You are NOT covered by any other health insurance program (except "permitted insurance" under current law)

The Essential First Step: Picking
The Right High-Deductible Health Plan

3

HSAs cannot be initiated unless a high-deductible health coverage plan is already in effect.

The confusing nature of health insurance plans in the American workplace can make it difficult to perform a true "apples to apples" comparison when you're shopping for any insurance plan. But the HSA program, if it does nothing else, provides a benchmark for coverage and care.

Under new rules recently signed into law, the benchmark is identified as a "qualified high-deductible health insurance policy." The rules of what can and cannot be covered are described in the law, and the rules regarding the deductible are also spelled out.

Why a High-Deductible Plan?

Prior experience with MSAs has shown that health-related savings plans work best when combined with an insurance policy that will cover what's known as a "catastrophic" medical condition. The law recognizes that no matter how much money a family puts aside in savings for health care, a single catastrophic event — a car crash, a house fire causing personal injury, a severe illness — could wipe out all those savings in a matter of weeks.

What's "Catastrophic Coverage"?

Catastrophic coverage is designed to help you in the event of — well, a catastrophe. If you're injured in a car accident, if you're diagnosed with a severe medical condition, if you have a premature baby — catastrophic coverage keeps health catastrophes from being financial catastrophes as well.

You'll also hear catastrophic coverage referred to as "indemnity" or "traditional" coverage. All three terms may be used with high-deductible health plans.

Qualification Rules Specified by Current Congressional Law:

- Deductible *minimums* of $1,000 for an individual, or $2,000 for a family plan.
- Out-of-pocket *maximums* not to exceed $5,100* for individuals, or $10,200* for families.
- No copays allowed (no "first dollar" coverage) until after the minimum deductible amount has been met.

* * Amount lixted is for 2005, indexed annually.

The low-cost high-deductible health insurance policy is there to pay the biggest bills, the bills that can accrue for a serious medical condition. HSA money is available for the smaller expenses. It's meant to be used to pay for routine care, such as a winter flu shot, new eyeglasses, the unexpected splinter or twisted ankle. With the program, both the small bills and the large bills are covered.

Not All High-Deductible Health Policies Qualify

Just because a plan falls within the guidelines for deductibles ($1,000 – $5,000 for individuals, $2,000 – $10,000 for families) doesn't mean it qualifies for the HSA program.

A lot of policy plans may have high deductibles, but they also stipulate some copays. This alone means that many PPO policies in place do not qualify, even if they waive copays for routine care, such as annual checkups.

Another common glitch is the "family deductible." Under a qualifying plan, the deductible is a per-family dollar amount. This is different from many older plans, which stipulated a per-person (or individual) deductible.

Qualifying high-deductible health plans' family deductibles *must* cover every dependent you wish to cover. Many older plans have per-person deductibles even under family coverage. These plans *don't* qualify for HSAs.

A qualifying family plan must have a deductible of at least $2,000, but no higher than $10,000, and it must cover every dependent you wish to include in the plan. It doesn't matter if you have one child or ten children. The deductible applies to medical expenses for all of them, in the aggregate. When looking at plans, make sure the deductible is a family deductible.

No Copays, But Some Coinsurance

Qualifying high-deductible health insurance polices do not allow for what's called "first dollar" coverage — in other words, the insurance company is not allowed to contribute any payment or reimbursement to the insured person until the deductible limit has been met.

However, the IRS currently permits some qualifying plans that stipulate that the insured person must also contribute for a percentage of doctor, hospital and prescription medicine fees *after* the deductible has been met. The amount you will be asked to pay might be 20 percent of the cost of the care. While this looks, feels and sounds like a copay, it's known as coinsurance. The difference between the two is that a copay is based on a fixed amount, while coinsurance is based on a fixed percentage.

Are you home-free after meeting your deductible? Not necessarily. Even under some qualifying plans, you could still pay a percentage (coinsurance) of your medical expenses after meeting your deductible. Choose carefully. Plans that require coinsurance after the deductible probably charge you a lower premium, so they might be a good choice for someone in good health who doesn't expect to meet the deductible. For someone who will have to meet the deductible, though, such a plan could get expensive.

Good plans have little or no coinsurance; lower-cost plans stipulate coinsurance for everything from a prescribed aspirin to a hospital stay, after the deductible has been met. You should shop carefully for the plan that best suits your ability to participate in paying for any extra costs after the deductible is met.

Out-of-Pocket Maximums for Coinsurance

Fortunately, even with some coinsurance you will not pay and pay and pay. The safety net is the law's limit for what are called **out-of-pocket expenses**. Out-of-pocket expenses are, in the broadest sense, any medical expenses you must pay for in the course of the year. (Whether a specific expense counts towards your out-of-pocket maximum depends on your medical coverage. Some network-based medical plans count your in-network spending separately from your out-of-network spending. Others may impose a monetary penalty if you fail to comply with preauthorization requirements — then double that penalty by not counting that money towards your out-of-pocket maximum. It pays to read the fine print!)

Safety Nets

Your high-deductible policy has two safety nets built in:
1. Your deductible, the point at which the plan starts paying for most of your health care
2. Your out-of-pocket maximum, the point at which you don't have to spend another dime on covered services until the end of the year.

With qualifying high-deductible health plans, the deductible counts toward the out-of-pocket maximum. You'll often encounter plans whose out-of-pocket maximum is simply double the deductible.

High-deductible policies that qualify under current law for HSAs not only limit the out-of-pocket maximum, but also include the deductible figure within that maximum. Under the law, in 2005 and indexed annually, the most you will pay out-of-pocket with an individual policy is $5,100, even if your deductible is $5,000, the most you will pay out-of-pocket for a family policy is $10,200, and this will include your family policy deductible amount and any coinsurance thereafter.

In practice, out-of-pocket maximums are usually double the amount of the deductible. When shopping for a policy, pay attention to the out-of-pocket maximum, and the coinsurance terms of your qualifying policy.

Lower-income families might find it a stretch to cover the worst-case scenario — thousands of dollars in coinsurance — during the first year of the program. In later years, as the HSA account builds up, it should contain plenty of accumulated funds, enough to cover the out-of-pocket maximum and any coinsurance fees incurred after deductibles have been met.

A worrisome question does come up for people who convert to an HSA-qualifying policy later in the tax year. They may not be able to deposit enough to cover six months or three months of a worst-case-scenario illness or accident. In recognition of this, some insurers may waive the deductible, or a portion of the deductible, for that first partial tax year. If you are switching policies, check to see if this waiver might apply to you.

Remember, in this transitional period, insurance companies are feeling their way around the marketplace, too. It is possible for you to negotiate with them for a better deal. Keep this in mind when talking with your broker or directly with the insurance company. (If you are a member of an employer's group high-deductible plan, you may have less negotiating power — your employer has already brokered the deal for you.)

Does My Existing HMO or PPO Qualify?

Fee-for-service insurance plans set up as Health Maintenance Organizations (HMOs) do not currently qualify for the HSA program. Federal and state restrictions relating to HMOs would have to be substantially changed first.

Anticipating Sticker Shock

When you first switch from an HMO to a high-deductible health plan, be prepared for "sticker shock." The first time you visit the doctor, you won't write a check afterwards for a $20 office-visit co-pay. You may wind up writing a check for $75 (if the doctor is in-network) or $240, or $375, or even $500 (if the doctor is out-of-network).

This can take some getting used to. After all, you're probably not used to thinking about how much health care really costs. Anticipate this first awkward moment with a starting balance in your HSA. More importantly, understand that your doctor visit did not suddenly get "more expensive." Remember that your employer has been subsidizing the bulk of doctor's fees on your behalf. Take another look at the preface to this book and remind yourself of the root causes of health care price increases: technological increases, new drugs, years of evolving legislation, a changing system. And take a deep breath, and look at your deductible. You've probably taken a big step towards meeting it with that first doctor visit.

Some of the old network plans (those known as Preferred Provider Options, or PPOs) can qualify under the law, provided they include high deductibles and no copays. Under these plans, you're given some incentive to only use services provided by doctors, specialists, and hospitals that are part of the network and have agreed to reimbursement rules the insurer has set up. And usually, there's a limit to how much you can spend on medical care outside of the network that will count towards your deductible. Under what's known as a "safe harbor" provision (as noted in IRS Notice 2004-23) a qualifying PPO is also allowed — although not required — to pay all costs for preventive care, such as annual checkups and cancer screenings.

A PPO may qualify for the HSA program even if it has two different deductible figures for out-of-network and in-network services, and if expenses for prescription drugs are included in the deductible as part of a prescription drug plan or rider. HSA regulations consider only the in-network deductible amount for services and medicines. Your annual contribution limit (the amount that may be deposited to your HSA in any given tax year) is determined by the in-network deductible for doctors and services.

A PPO's annual deductible for out-of-network services is not taken into account in setting an individual's contribution limit. This will be true even if the individual's out-of-pocket expense limit for services outside of that PPO's network is higher than the out-of-pocket maximum allowed for HSAs — $2,650 for individuals, and $5,250 for family coverage.

PPOs that qualify for HSAs generally provide you with good incentives to use care providers who are in-network. But you can still use HSA funds to visit a doctor or specialist you choose. That's right: it's your choice to go to whomever you wish, wherever you wish. You can take your HSA funds and visit a doctor in another state, or go to the world-renowned Mayo Clinic in Minnesota if you think you need to go there.

With an HSA, because you control how you spend the account, you have freedom to see any health care provider you wish. You might pay a little more for it, but even so, what you pay will be tax-free.

How Do I Buy a High-Deductible Insurance Policy?

A qualified policy can be purchased either as an individual plan or through a group plan. You can purchase policies online, or through an insurance broker. Brokers usually represent a single insurance firm, though an "independent" broker may sell plans from different companies. Insurance "agents" may be independent, or may work with a brokerage company or for a specific insurer, such as Aetna or United Healthcare.

Many of the larger insurance companies are putting together new plans specifically to attract people who want to start HSAs. You can expect to see many new offerings for individuals and for small businesses, from both old, established insurers, and from those new to the field.

Because insurance providers and financial companies expect consumer-directed health care to surge by the end of this decade, many unusual venues are springing up to offer high-deductible health insurance plans and HSAs directly to consumers. For example, Sam's Club, the cut-rate discounter known for its big-box stores and jumping auction website, sells insurance online, specifically targeting individual policyholders and small businesses.

From the Databank: They Can Get It for You Wholesale

Sam's Club has begun selling health insurance for small businesses in Missouri and nine other states, offering the insurance through several carriers as of February 2004.

Through an affiliation with insurance broker Answer Financial Inc., Sam's Club will initially offer the insurance to its members in Missouri, Illinois, California, North Carolina, Ohio, Tennessee, Georgia, Iowa, Indiana, and Wisconsin.

In a news release, Sam's said its policy plans are targeted to companies with fewer than 100 employees; the plans offer a range of deductibles, coinsurance, and out-of-pocket limits. Sam's has offered auto, health and business insurance products through its website for several years and will administer the health insurance from its Bentonville, Ark., headquarters.

Source: *Kansas City Business Journal*

Individual or Group Coverage?

If you're self-employed and own a sole proprietorship, you'll face higher costs if you choose a plan on your own. If you're self-employed and currently uninsured, the hurdles for getting a policy by yourself are huge. In most states, insurance companies must accept you if you have been insured during the previous 12 months. If you have not, they may set conditions or exemptions. Nonetheless, it doesn't hurt to try, and many previously uninsured individuals may find HSAs the road to becoming insured at reasonable cost.

Trade associations, local business groups, and state and local governments may offer you the chance to join a "pool" of individuals in a group plan. If such a group plan offers a qualifying high-deductible policy, this may be a good route.

Among state governments, there's a slow but growing movement to offer HSA-qualified health plans to serve underinsured small businesses and self-employed individuals. In New York, for example, there's a state program called HealthyNY (www.HealthyNY.com) available for sole proprietors and for companies with fewer than 50 employees. HealthyNY does not offer a qualified high-deductible policy at the present time, but expects to have one in place by 2005.

Individual or Family Plan?

If your family includes two working adults — spouses or legally recognized domestic partners — you can both purchase individual high-deductible health insurance policies that will qualify both of you for HSAs. This isn't often done, simply because it can be cheaper to purchase a family policy to cover both adults. But it can be done, and it may be an option to consider if one adult has greater medical needs than the other, or if both adults maintain their own small businesses. Alternatively, if one partner has a plan that does not qualify, the other partner may choose to opt for a HSA through which he or she may be able to fund copayments of the other partner. (See following page.)

If your family includes dependent children, one of you might opt for an individual policy; the other can still choose a family deductible policy to cover the rest of the clan.

What? No Co-Pay?

A health care future without co-pays isn't as bleak — or as unusual — as it seems. Think about what you're currently paying for auto or home insurance, and what deductibles you chose. Most car owners think nothing of carrying a $500 or $1,000 deductible when insuring their cars, and a $5,000 deductible on homeowner's insurance is fairly standard. In fact, many choose higher deductibles for this type of insurance to keep their premium costs low.

Drivers don't expect their car insurance to cover the replacement of a flat tire, and homeowners rarely invoke their policies for damages they feel they can afford to pay for, such as broken windows or a plumbing problem. These forms of insurance seem to work better when you rely upon them for serious or catastrophic events. With HSAs, you take a similar responsibility when paying for health care, participating to the limit that feels affordable, under a high-deductible health insurance policy that covers catastrophic medical need.

Here's a common situation: one spouse currently has no insurance. The other currently has an insurance policy through a large corporate employer. The spouse who is already insured has several options:
1. Adding the uninsured spouse to the corporate policy.
2. Letting the uninsured spouse get an individual high deductible insurance policy.
3. Dropping the corporate plan altogether to obtain a high-- deductible, family plan that covers both adults.

Answer 1 seems like a no-brainer — unless adding a second adult to the corporate policy requires an additional premium, which is payable to the first spouse's employer. It may prove less costly to let the uninsured spouse pay for his or her own high-deductible health insurance policy, out of the couple's joint income, than to let the additional premium costs take a bigger bite of the first spouse's paycheck.

When dependent children are added to the mix, the choices will include assigning them to one policy or the other. If you've done the worksheets in Chapter 2, you have some idea of your past and estimated future costs for family health care. Review these numbers, and have them at hand when you shop for a health insurance provider.

Remember, too, that you can use funds from your HSA to pay for the eligible medical expenses of any immediate family member — even if you're the only one who qualifies to open and contribute to an HSA.

Employees with Families

If you have children or other dependents to care for, you may be fearful about switching from a low-deductible PPO or first-dollar HMO policy to a high-deductible heath insurance policy plan. Low-paid employees, especially, cling to the myth of the co-pay. And it's true that for many, paying the first $2,000 in medical expenses (to cover the lowest family deductible allowed) might be a financial hardship.

However, those whose income is lowest may stand to gain the most from the combination of HSAs and high-deductible health plans. Not only will your HSA contributions lower the amount of income you pay tax on, but they may also nudge you into a lower tax bracket, so you pay less tax on all your income. By lowering their taxable income this way, some individuals and families could qualify for the Earned Income Tax Credit — a tax-time bonus that could make a difference of thousands of dollars. So although $2,000 in health care expenses seems like a lot at first, in the long run it can pay for itself.

Employees with Poor Health History

What if you have pre-existing conditions, chronic illnesses, or special needs? You may at first be reluctant to switch to a high-deductible policy plan.

Paradoxically, you may benefit the most quickly from switching to a high-deductible health policy plan. You might meet the deductible than out-of-pocket maximum early in the year, and the policy pays for all medical expenses after that, with no further out-of-pocket cost to you.

You may already be paying large sums of money for co-pays. You may even be in debt trying to cover a hospital co-pay (which can cost as much as $500 in many PPO plans). Go through Worksheet #1 (from Chapter 2) and look at your true costs for health care.

And what if a specific care provider (such as a pediatric specialist or oncologist) isn't in the network for your new plan? In this case, the broader inclusions the HSA program allows for qualified medical expenses may allow you to keep going to the same specialist. And if your new plan is with your previous insurer — as is likely if you depend on employer-sponsored coverage — you should be able to enjoy uninterrupted coverage for your condition even if you switch from your old HMO to the new high-deductible plan.

Profile: Barbara and Greg

Barbara, a 53-year-old professor with tenure, is married to Greg, a lawyer, 55, who has worked for only two companies in his entire career. Their income looks pretty stable, but Barbara is nervous. She teaches at a state university — one of the schools whose funding has been cut lately — and she worries that it will eventually scale back the retiree medical benefits she's been counting on.

They have been pretty diligent about saving for retirement, their house will be paid off in a year, and they're not too worried about having income to support them when they've both stopped working. But Barbara's father died of Alzheimer's after a 10-year struggle with the disease, and she remembers all too well how caring for him sapped her mother's energy — and her financial resources. If she and Greg don't remain as healthy as they are now — and especially if she winds up without a generous retiree medical package — they may not have as much retirement income as they want.

Barbara and Greg have both been covered for years under the university's HMO. The plan has been generous, but lately its premiums and copayments have been rising fast. They've especially noticed the difference when they pay for Greg's brand-name ulcer medication — they've gone from $15 per refill to $75 per refill in just three years. If the plan's prices keep rising like this, Barbara estimates she and Greg will have trouble paying for their health care within four or five years.

They decide to try the combination of a high-deductible health plan and health savings account, just for one year (2005). If they don't like it, they can go back to the HMO next year. They choose a plan with a $6,000 family deductible because they want to contribute as much as they can to the HSA. (In their case, the maximum is $5,650, because Greg's age qualifies him to make a catch-up contribution.) The plan includes a prescription drug discount card; that eases some of their fears about Greg's medication, which is easily their largest and most constant medical expense.

They'll fund the HSA with Greg's year-end bonus — and he sure doesn't mind getting a tax break on that money. They don't expect to reach the deductible, but even if they do, there won't be a significant difference between that amount and what they're spending now for the HMO premiums. At *worst,* they'll probably wind up with some modest extra retirement savings. And their income taxes are lower too.

FINDING A VENDOR FOR QUALIFIED HIGH-DEDUCTIBLE PLANS

Because health insurance regulations vary state by state, the rollout of HSA-compatible policies has not yet reached all states.

If you're in Arizona, California, Colorado, Florida, Georgia, Illinois, Iowa, Michigan, Nevada, Ohio, Tennessee Texas and Utah, you'll have no trouble locating suitable high-deductible plans. In these states, major insurers, such as Nationwide, Blue Cross Blue Shield, Aetna, Cigna and United Healthcare offer an assortment of high-deductible plans, and will be rolling out additional offerings.

In states such as New York, Pennsylvania, New Jersey, and Massachusetts, it can be difficult to locate a qualifying high-deductible plan. As of this writing, there are no fewer than 15 plans before the insurance commissioners of these states, but major insurers have been slow to offer such products and have pretty much left the field to smaller firms.

In Pennsylvania for example, Golden Rule — a small, innovative insurance company that is now a part of United Healthcare — has taken the lead. Golden Rule was one of the first insurers to participate in MSAs and thus has a track record in servicing small businesses with qualifying high-deductible plans.

In New York, among the companies licensed to sell health insurance as of this writing offering a good product is PerfectHealth, which began writing HSA-qualifying high-deductible polices early in 2004.

To find out if there is a qualified HSA carrier in your state, see www.hsafinder.com for the latest updates and information.

You're Not On Your Own
Resources for information on plan vendors:
- A.M. Best
- The National Committee for Quality Assurance
- State Licensing Agencies
- The Better Business Bureau
- HSAfinder.com

Using Rating Services

Just like the auto industry has J.D. Powers, and the bond industry has Standard & Poor's and Moody's, the insurance industry has rating services that monitor customer satisfaction. Two recommended services are accessible on the Web:

A.M. Best (www.ambest.com)

You can access ratings for any company found in the database after you register online. There is no fee for registration, and only general information (such as your name and address) is required. If you want to receive junk mail and e-mail alerts, you have the choice to opt in for that, and the website is constantly updated with insurance industry news. The firm itself is more than a century old, and is the publisher of *Best's Review* and other publications.

Best's rates the companies based on their assets, corporate stability, and capability to pay out claims. For insurers found on the Web, Best's provides a "seal of approval" icon for companies rated as the most secure (ratings of A++, A+, A, A-, B++, B+). Along with well-established insurers, some of the early smaller companies in the HSA field, such as Golden Rule, are also rated by Best's.

NCQA (www.ncqa.org)

The National Committee for Quality Assurance (NCQA) is an independent nonprofit 501(c)(3) organization that measures consumer satisfaction with insurance companies. The organization puts out a report card on companies and provides "accreditation" to insurers that meet its requirements. High ratings go to companies with good track records for handling claims and swift reimbursements. Not all companies are interested in applying for NCQA's blessing, and since it's voluntary and relatively new (founded in 2000) you may not find your target company listed here. New companies sometimes appear on the website's "Status List" if they are waiting for accreditation.

Many of the nation's biggest insurers, including Blue Shield and Aetna, do participate. Since even these companies' plans vary in terms of service from state to state, a very good feature of this website is that it rates plans individually, and breaks them down by product line. No registration is required to view the ratings on this site.

State Licensing Agencies

While companies may be national, you can only buy insurance from a company licensed in your state to sell insurance. Any vendor you speak with should be able to provide proof of a current license.

If in doubt, contact your state government (by phone or Web) to locate the insurance department; then verify the license before you sign on the dotted line. The state agency should also be able to tell you if the vendor has any complaints pending or on file.

Why Choose a Smaller Firm at All?

Why bother to choose anything but a major insurance company?

The sad truth is that if you are self-employed and a sole proprietor, a major insurance company may not want your business. You may be small potatoes to them — or you may be, in their estimation, uninsurable. This is particularly true if you have not had a health insurance policy in force within the last year.

Big insurance companies really only want you if you're healthy and wealthy. They'd prefer you come to them already nicely insured, just ready to transfer your premium payments to their coffers. For example, you can't even apply for Blue Cross or Blue Shield in most states unless you can prove some other company has successfully insured you for 18 months. If you've been an entrepreneur without any health insurance since your college years, or if you let your COBRA lapse because the premiums cost too much — you're out of luck.

Big insurance companies will also charge you more, even for high-deductible policies. They may advertise what seem to be comparatively low rates, but their application forms usually state that, upon reviewing your application, they will reserve the right to offer you a slightly different plan at a higher premium cost. Even major companies are quite up-front about their propensity to "bait and switch."

All companies also reserve the right to "decline" coverage. While some states require insurers to service businesses with three or more employees, there's no law, state or federal, that says an insurance company has to provide service to every person who applies for an individual policy.

Definitions:

COBRA refers to the Consolidated Omnibus Budget Reconciliation Act.
HIPAA stands for Health Insurance Portability and Accountability Act.
Both laws are designed to make it easier for you to get coverage and keep coverage. HIPAA also safeguards the privacy of your medical information — as you've probably noticed if you've purchased a prescription or sought medical care lately. HIPAA, like most of health care, means yet another form for you to sign.

Common Age and Residency Proof Requirements:

- Covered individuals must be 64 1/2 years old or YOUNGER.
- Dependent children must be 19–23 or YOUNGER (varies by state).
- Covered individuals must be permanent state residents.
- Covered individuals must be legal residents of the U.S. for a certain period (usually three months).

Can I Be Rejected?

Unfortunately, yes. Applications for individual policies are not approved automatically. Individuals who smoke or have existing serious medical problems may find it harder to find a reputable vendor.* And if you've been rejected once, it can be even harder to get approval the second time.

People who have an existing policy in place can use that as proof of their insurability. If a plan has recently expired (such as a COBRA continuation policy at the end of its term) the "termination of policy" document you received in the mail may be useful as proof of prior insurance. Under a federal law called the Health Insurance Portability and Accountability Act of 1997, or HIPAA, when your coverage ends, the plan must issue you a "Certificate of Creditable Coverage," which proves you have been insured.

*Note: Though certain behaviors and conditions may reduce your "insurability" — that is, they make you likelier to incur large medical costs, and therefore a worse risk for an insurance company to take on — it's inadvisable to lie to them, or even to omit relevant information, when you apply for coverage. For one thing, even if you are accepted for coverage, you can't hide your subsequent medical spending patterns from your insurance company. If they discover your fraud, you're likely to find yourself without coverage — at the very least. And if you've purchased your policy through your employer, beware — many employers consider this behavior grounds for termination.

What if I Have a "Pre-existing Condition"?

A "pre-existing condition" is a medical condition (ailment or injury) that was either diagnosed or treated before you apply for a new policy plan. Most new insurance policies will not cover new treatments for the same illness or injury until a "waiting period" has elapsed. This period can range from three months to 12 months.

Under HIPAA, a pre-existing condition must be covered without a waiting period if you have already been insured (by someone else) through all the previous 12 months. If you don't have existing insurance, the longest you will have to wait to cover the pre-existing condition under your new plan is 12 months.

Example: The Young Entrepreneur
Bill, 30, a graphic designer, has been working for a large corporation

for three years, and he's been covered by that firm's PPO. Bill is in decent shape, but he has asthma, and he spends several hundred dollars a year in prescription copayments for his maintenance inhalers. The inhalers are name-brand drugs — without insurance, they'd cost him several *thousand* dollars a year.

Bill decides to open his own studio. He gives his two weeks' notice, and applies for individual PPO coverage. But in his last week of work, the bombshell drops: the PPO has declined to cover him.

Bill does some quick calculations: first, what his asthma medicine would cost him if he had to pay for it all himself over 12 months; second, what it would cost him to continue his employer coverage through COBRA while he's finding individual coverage. Because he knows he has less chance of being turned down again, he decides to apply for a high-deductible policy, and chooses COBRA coverage for the time being.

One month later, Bill's high-deductible coverage is in force and he has established an HSA account. Because he opted for a month of COBRA coverage, his health insurance has been continuous, and his new plan will cover his asthma. He can save on the costs of his medication, and pay for his month of COBRA tax-free.

COBRA coverage is considered temporary relief coverage and — depending on certain restrictions — can qualify you to open an HSA, regardless of what kind of plan you are continuing. See Chapter Eight for more details.

Age and Residency Requirements

Age and residency requirements are common to all plans, but also vary from state to state. Generally, plans won't take you if you're 65 or older (or if you otherwise qualify for Medicare or Medicaid). The upper age limit for dependent children ranges from 19 to 23, depending on the state and whether the child is a full-time student. When you apply for insurance, you may be asked to provide proof of the ages and residency status for yourself and for all family members who will be covered under the new policy.

FINDING A POLICY PROVIDER FOR YOUR SMALL BUSINESS

If you're self-employed, you may already have a broker or agent for your other business insurance needs: they are the same professionals who sold you policies for liability and property insurance. These companies may or may not handle health insurance. If not, ask them to recommend a health insurance broker to you.

When asking for referrals, specifically ask for vendors with experience in the small business market. You might also ask colleagues or those in related businesses to refer an insurance broker or agent to you. Once you've got their names and their numbers, just call them and ask if they offer any HSA-qualified high-deductible coverage plans. If they say "yes," all you have to do is mention you are reviewing health insurance providers, and would like to see what they can present. If they say no, move on the next referral.

If you run out of leads, try the Yellow Pages of your local phone book. Good agents are licensed and certified. They have a professional designation, such as Registered Health Underwriter (RHU) or Registered Employee Benefits Consultant (REBC), or hold membership in the National Association of Health Insurance Agents (AHIA) or National Association of Insurance and Financial Advisors (NAIFA).

Most Popular Sources for Information:

Overwhelmingly, people who need information about health care gravitate to two resources: their friends and family; and the Internet. Both can be good sources of information. Just make sure you're getting the truth! In this, as in all buying decisions, it pays to double-check.

When you sit down with an agent, you can use the data collected for Worksheet 1 in Chapter 2 to collaborate on which policy will be the most cost-effective given your situation. Be honest with your agent or broker. Don't withhold important information. If a dependent had a heart operation two years ago, or you yourself have a pre-existing condition, be prepared to discuss this with the agent.

You will have to fill out applications completely and accurately. If any applications are incomplete or inaccurate, the company may either refuse to pay your claims or cancel your policy.

It's best to check with at least three vendors and get at least three competitive bids for high-deductible policies. Get each bid broken down into inclusions and exclusions — that is, what the policy will and won't cover — so you can compare them at leisure.

A Potential Problem with Brokers

Some brokers won't even tell you about high-deductible health plans unless you ask — and even then, they might not be happy about it. Why?

It's simple: brokers work on commission. The more expensive the health plan, the bigger the commission. Since high-deductible health plans are drastically less expensive than other plans, brokers typically don't recommend them. So — particularly if you're looking for individual coverage — you may find an online brokerage or vendor more appealing.

Reputable insurance providers should provide you with:
- Premium schedule (dates premium payments are due)
- Benefits schedule (detailed list of what is or is not covered)
- Premium rates and ALL applicable administrative fees (monthly and setup fees)
- Copy of a sample agreement and application form (to review before you sign up)
- Checkable references from other clients with similar needs

When you buy a policy, the first premium is usually due at the time you sign the purchase agreement. The amount you write the check for will also include monthly administrative fees, and perhaps an initial setup fee as well.

Remember that direct agents, independent agents, and brokers all get a commission on the policies they sell. No matter how nice your agent may seem, he or she will try to steer you to a more expensive policy.

From the Databank: Health Insurance Fraud Is on the Rise

Federal investigators are sounding the alarm about a sharp rise in health insurance fraud schemes specifically targeted to small businesses and the self-employed. In a March 2004 report to Senator Charles Grassley (R-Iowa), the

General Accounting Office identified 144 bogus insurance companies who had bilked more than 15,000 small employers, taking in policy premium payments and then disappearing when claims were presented. Some 200,000 policyholders, many of them self-employed or workers in food service or construction, were left stranded with at least $252 million in medical bills left unpaid.

The GAO said at least five bogus insurers were found in every state. Alabama, Florida, Illinois, New Jersey, North Carolina and Texas had the most offenders — more than 25 bogus firms each. The companies generally advertised extremely low rates to draw in subscribers who failed to notice that the companies were not state-licensed to issue insurance plans. After taking in premium payments for several months, the sham companies would simply close down, change names and move to another state. Small businesses that purchased policies through an association or business group were not safe; one-fourth of those bilked were associations who failed to check licensing before promoting the plans to their association members.

Source: *The New York Times*, March 3, 2004.

Should You Switch Providers?

If your agent or broker doesn't know about HSAs (and many do not), don't be alarmed; they are quite new. Instead, ask to be referred to a colleague who DOES know about HSA-compatible products. Inform your contact that you are going to be shopping for a provider that offers a qualified product, and give them a firm deadline to get back to you with a new bid that includes at least one qualifying high-deductible health insurance plan.

Dealing with Resistance

When you announce that you are shopping for an HSA-compatible policy, don't expect your current insurer to be happy. Insurance companies make more money on the higher premiums paid for full-coverage plans; they have had, in the past, little incentive to even research high-deductible plans on your behalf.

If you've done the worksheet in Chapter 2, you'll have some hard numbers to let them know why this is important to you. It pays you to shop for the best plan at the best price.

If you've done your homework, and have looked at high-deductible plans from other vendors, you'll have a stronger case when trying to convince your current provider that you will drop them — if you have to.

COMPARING HIGH-DEDUCTIBLE PLANS

Whether you are self-employed or choosing a plan from your employer's offerings, the premium price alone should not dictate which high-deductible plan you pick.

When comparing plans from vendor to vendor, examine each to see what services are covered, and which are not. Every plan will have certain exclusions. Even though HSA funds can pay for expenses not covered by your plan, certain kinds of medical expenses may not be covered or may not count towards your deductible.

The best kind of "hit by a truck" insurance covers illness as well as accidents, hospitalization as well as surgery and care when you get home. Check to see how the plan defines "emergency care." What conditions are considered emergencies? Chest pains? Profuse bleeding?

Another thing to check is the "lifetime maximum benefit" the insurer guarantees to pay. The lifetime maximum is just what it sounds like: the most the insurer will pay for your care in your lifetime. A respectable figure is around $5,000,000. That's what the majority of plans offer. A $1,000,000 cap offered in exchange for a cheaper premium may be no bargain, since a single hospital stay after a surgery can cost hundreds of thousands of dollars.

The sad truth is that the better a plan is, the more expensive it will be. Policies costing less than $100 per month (for an individual) cannot really be a substitute for a more generous and comprehensive medical policy that covers more of the costs of care. Many small businesses have suffered when their health care has proven inadequate to cover an employee's catastrophic illness. If you are self-employed, having a lifetime cap that is too low could put your business and family in jeopardy.

A Quick Checklist
When you're comparing high-deductible plans, pay special attention to the following:
- Out-of-pocket maximums
- Definitions of "emergency" and emergency care
- Lifetime maximums
- Excluded services
- Limitations

- Coverage of services (such as psychiatric care or trips to the chiropractor) with particular relevance to your health
- Renewability
- Coverage away from home
- Requirements for preauthorizing services
- Customer service ratings
- Provider networks

Consider, too, your own experience of getting this information from the plan. Was it easy to find? Did you have problems navigating the plan's website? Did you have to spend a long time on hold before someone could answer your questions?

It will take some time, but you may want to look at your worksheet from Chapter 2 and see how your expenses would be covered under the different plans available to you. For example, under an employer-sponsored PPO, your copayment for talking to the doctor about controlling your type-II diabetes would likely be low, and your prescription copayments might be manageable. But when you factor in your monthly premiums — and the cost of the treadmill you bought on the doctor's recommendation — it might stop looking like such a bargain. By contrast, under a high-deductible policy with an HSA, you'd have to pay the full cost of that office visit, as well as the cost of your prescriptions up to your deductible. But your premiums would be far lower, you could pay for that treadmill tax-free, and you might have enough left over to start earning investment income for the future.

Picking the right plan is always a matter of trade-offs. It's up to you to find the best balance for your situation. Taking the time to make an informed decision now could save you thousands in the years to come.

Common Exclusions

Generally, high-deductible plans do not cover dental or vision care unless the need arises from an accident, injury or disease. Because HSAs can cover routine dental and vision care (including checkups, cleaning, X-rays, new eyeglasses and contact lenses) this exclusion is not a problem for most.

Other exclusions are common throughout the industry (see box on the next page) and appear in most policies. By comparing exclusions on different policy plans, you can easily see which policies are generous,

---

Common Exclusions and Limitations

- Any services provided by a government body (state, federal, city, county, or foreign).
- Any services provided by a relative by blood, marriage, or adoption.
- Any services performed prior to the beginning of the policy.

---

and which are stingier, in terms of coverage.

Are you are planning to start a new family? If not, then you may not need a plan with maternity benefits. Other coverage that may be optional for you might be psychiatric care, drug and alcohol treatment, or outpatient therapies such as acupuncture. Choosing a plan without these options usually will cost less.

Looking ahead to the long term, try to factor in lifestyle changes you might anticipate five years or ten years down the road. If some of your blood relatives have chronic health problems, such as diabetes or heart disease, arthritis, cataracts, or if you are in a risk group for cancer, make sure that common treatments for these conditions will be covered adequately by your plan.

Guarantee Renewability

If you're purchasing a policy on your own, you've spent a lot of time on this decision. You don't want to have to do it again soon. So, make sure the policy is "guaranteed renewable." *Get this in writing.* This means that the insurer will not be able to, at a whim, cancel your policy, as long as you continue to pay the premiums on time. If possible, also get a cap on percentage increases over the first three years. This can mean a lot if a sudden illness hits one or more family members.

Coverage Out of State

Does your coverage travel? If you travel a lot on business, have a second home, or have children attending colleges or schools outside of your home state, investigate options to assure your policy extends to medical care — not just emergency care — in these other places.

Care Management Policies

You'll also want to examine what your policy requires of you in terms of "utilization review." This tells you whether or not you need to get preauthorized permission for certain kinds of surgeries, or whether you need written permission (a note from your doctor, usually called a "referral") to see a specialist. Some plans use the term "precertification"; it means the same thing.

While it's true that you can use your HSA dollars to get help from any medical care professional who qualifies under IRS rules (see Chapter 6), whether or not you stay within utilization guidelines may affect what's counted towards your deductible and what is not. Some plans even penalize you — usually by raising the amount you must pay before they cover the expense — if you seek major care without preauthorizing it. Since the government allows insurers some leeway in this area, check your plan offerings carefully to see how much leeway you have as well. Once the deductible is met, you can still get help from the care professional of your choice; but coverage and pricing is plan dependent so, again, check your plan offering carefully.

Know What Your Plan Requires

Be a smart consumer. Health care expenses are unavoidable, but bureaucratic expenses — such as preauthorization penalties — can usually be sidestepped if you take the time to familiarize yourself with your plan.

Customer Service

An April, 2004 Small Business Survey of more than 1,200 small businesses showed that 72% of the 1,200 respondents relied on brokers in choosing a health care plan. The survey also indicated respondents sought outside input beyond their broker about a third of the time. Often this meant checking references to see if current customers were satisfied with the vendor.

Some questions to ask include: How does the insurer handle problems and claims? Are payments prompt or sluggish? Can you check account and claim status by telephone or Web? Are current clients satisfied with service? Ask for references, and take some time to check

them out.
Before You Sign on the Dotted Line...

Read the policy. Have someone else look at it. Make sure you're getting what you asked for. To satisfy any concerns about the company's
financial stability and reliable customer service, check with your state's
licensing board. If you have any questions about how your policy will
work, contact the company or the agent before you sign.

Key Financial Considerations for Any Policy Plan

1. Cost of premium(s) on monthly basis for the year.
2. Amount of deductible for year.
3. Maximum lifetime benefit amount for life of the policyholder.
4. Exclusion of preventive care from deductible amounts.
5. Discounts for use of in-network services or doctors.
6. Additional costs for desirable options (e.g., maternity, prescription
   drug benefits).
7. Guaranteed renewability.
8. Reasonable assurance of insurer's financial stability and ability to
   pay claims.
9. Insurer's reputation for good customer service and rapid response to
   questions when they arise.

You will find the first seven parameters answered by the policy itself;
to satisfy your concerns about the company's financial stability and
reliable customer service, check with your state's licensing board
before you sign.

Here are three more good rules of thumb to keep in mind when choosing a vendor:
Companies with good reputations generally earn them and try to keep
them.
Capping expenses for the next three years is more important than getting the cheapest rate this year.
High-quality health care is still the main objective. Keep it in mind
at all times.

Health Insurance Checklist
Good plans should cover:
- Inpatient hospital services
- Outpatient surgery
- Emergency services
- Physician visits (in the hospital)
- Office visits
- Care by specialists
- Skilled nursing care
- Medical tests and X-rays
- Preventive care and checkups

Good plans may or may not cover these options:
- Prescription drugs
- Mental health care
- Drug and alcohol abuse treatment
- Home health care visits
- Rehabilitation facility care
- Physical therapy
- Hospice care
- Maternity care
- Chiropractic care
- Alternative health care (such as acupuncture or chiropractic
        medicine)
-Well-baby care

The best plans may waive the deductible for preventive care, and effectively pay 100 percent of all costs for routine procedures, such as annual physicals, age-appropriate cancer screenings, pre-natal care, and required immunizations for children covered by the policy.

HSA QUALIFYING HEALTH PLANS: THE BASICS

What Is a Qualifying High-Deductible Health Plan?

- A qualified high-deductible plan may be obtained through an employer or purchased by an individual.

- A qualifying plan has a minimum annual deductible of at least $1,000 for an individual or $2,000 for a family (*indexed annually).

- The minimum annual deductible applies to in-network benefits only.

- The total sum of deductible and required out-of-pocket coinsurance fees cannot exceed $5,100 for individual or $10,200 for a family (*indexed annually).

- Higher out-of-pocket limits are permitted for out-of-network services.

- Doctor visits and prescription drugs (see Note) are covered like other expenses, subject to the annual deductible, not with copays.

Note:s Pending changes in IRS rules, fee waivers may be permitted for certain types of preventative care, such as mammograms and child immunizations. Transition relief in 2004 and 2005 authorized by the IRS will allow qualifying high-deductible plans for individuals already participating in programs with a prescription rider or separate drug plan that pays only benefits for prescription drugs before the deductible is satisfied. For more information, see IRS Notice 2004-

Establishing a Health Savings Account

4

This chapter covers the legal requirements for a qualified account that you can use for your deposits and withdrawals for medical care.

As 2004 was the first year HSAs were allowed, the small sums of money involved suggest that most people's first account will be in the form of an interest-bearing checking account. In later years, as funds accumulate, people will want to put their HSA dollars into accounts that offer higher rates of interest. Like IRAs and Keogh accounts, an HSA account is completely portable — you can transfer it at will from one bank to the next if you think the move will give you better return or better service.

This year, your HSA balance will be small, and the account will behave much like a checking account. As the account grows, however, you'll probably want to treat it more like an investment vehicle, and move it into an account that offers a higher interest rate.

As with IRAs, HSA investors can have multiple accounts in more than one bank. The only limitation is this: even if you spread your HSA dollars into more than one account, the amount you can put away is still limited by your annual contribution limit — the amount of your annual deductible. (Yes, that's another reason why the high-deductible policy must be "in effect" before you can open a health savings account.)

Multiple Accounts

If you have a $1,500 deductible on your health insurance policy, you can open one $1,500 HSA, two $750 HSAs, three $500 HSAs — it's up to you. You'll probably pay more in account administration fees. And you'll be the one who has to make sure that your deposits don't exceed federal limits. But as your accounts grow, you may want to make sure that these investments are diversified — that is, that not all of your money is in the same place.

A good HSA account will have the following features:

- Easy deposits — in person, by mail, by electronic transfer, or through an automatic payroll deposit mechanism.
- Easy withdrawals: you can use a checkbook or debit card for payments; some people will use checks for larger expenses (doctor fees) and the debit card for smaller expenses (drugstore prescriptions).
- An attractive daily compound interest rate on your deposits (2 percent APR is the current norm).
- Reasonable monthly charges for administering the account (annual fees under 2 percent are reported as the norm, although some vendors offer "no fee" accounts to attract depositors).
- Ability to check balances and recent account action at any time, by phone, by web and by monthly printed account summaries.
- Yearly printed statement of all deposits and detailed data on all debits or expenses, to satisfy the IRS requirements for reporting (See "Rules for Reporting...," on page 136, for more information).

Trends in this newer form of banking include products from major credit card companies, tying in automated tracking of expenses, prescription drug discounts, and point or cash-back bonus programs.

Who Offers HSAs Today?

As with HSA-qualified insurance policies, the rollout is state-by-state. By the end of this tax year, there will be thousands of players in the game.

Large, well-known, nationwide financial companies such as Merrill Lynch and Fidelity are rolling out HSA products, but slowly. Smaller firms, such as American Chartered Bank in Illinois, offer free accounts and pursue this market more aggressively.

Yes, there is a danger that "fly-by-night" operators may flood the market early on, but provide inadequate resources. On the other hand, institutions already experienced with Archer or Medical Savings Account (MSAs) are expanding the number of states and insurance providers they serve. When you're choosing among provider companies, follow a few basic rules. (To get you started, a listing of custodians appears on the companion website to this book, www.HSAfinder.com.)

Account Custodians You May Consider:
- Banks
- Insurance companies
- Your current retirement account custodians
- Even an individual, if he or she satisfies certain requirements

---

Who Can Be an "Account Custodian"?

Under current federal HSA regulations, just about any bank or insurance company can become a custodian of your money and your HSA account. The law is quite broad, as even a single person can be the custodian if he or she demonstrates "suitability" to the satisfaction of the office of the Secretary of the U.S. Treasury. This allows for most of the financial institutions now acting as custodians for people's IRA, Keogh and 401(k) dollars to get in into the HSA business.

On the one hand, that's good. These firms have experience in handling retirement accounts, and offer many different levels of service to a variety of consumers — no matter how much or how little you have to invest. These companies also compete for the right to manage your retirement account, and they usually compete by trying to improve products, or service levels, or the rate of return (better interest rates on your money).

On the other hand, it also allows for some finagling by firms and individuals who might meet the "suitability" bar but have no track record in handling consumer investments. The door is open for the same fly-by-night operators who thrive on boiler-room stock and bond schemes. It also allows health insurance companies to set up banking partnerships or HSA side businesses, even though they've had little experience in helping consumers create wealth. When you pay into a

Federal Requirements for the Custodian Institution

- The custodian can be a bank, an insurance company, a business or a person who demonstrates "suitability" to the Secretary of the U.S. Treasury*.
- The custodian must be registered with the IRS as an HSA custodian.
- The custodian cannot be invested in life insurance contracts, or sell life insurance policies.
- Assets and holdings from people's HSA accounts must stay separate from the company's other asset properties (with some exceptions for mutual funds).
- Money paid into HSA accounts is fully vested, and cannot be removed by employers or forfeited by employees.
- Administrative fees (such as monthly fees) and setup fees are permitted.

* *Banks as defined by the Section 408(n) and insurance companies as defined by Section 816 of the U.S. Tax Code.*

health insurance company, you don't expect to get return and interest back. And they're not used to paying out a return to you.

Buyer Beware
Watch out for:
- Custodians with no track record of *any* consumer investments
- "Fly-by-nighters" (check custodians' names and reputations with or the Better Business Bureau)
- Hidden fees or fees that seem higher than the competition
- Custodians without FDIC insurance
HSAs are so new that *no* companies have long-standing track records in handling them. But that doesn't mean you have to go in blindly. You can still look at a potential custodian's record with other forms of consumer investments.

The insurance giant Fortis, for example, offers HSAs in Indiana and Illinois, through a subsidiary, Fortis HSA Trustee Services; there is a single application form for the account and for the health insurance. While fees are waived for the account the first year, it remains to be seen if account fees in future years will stay competitive with other trustees.

Paradoxically, the one type of insurance company that is experienced in long-term investments is specifically excluded from peddling HSAs. These are the companies that sell life insurance — long-term investments and annuities that do bear interest over the life of the policyholder, and pay benefits on the policyholder's death. Such an organization is usually defined as an insurance company under a section of the U.S. Tax Code.

All custodians must be registered with the Internal Revenue Service, as they will be responsible for reports that verify deposits (called "contributions") and withdrawals (called "distributions"). This is similar to the rules for custodians who oversee retirement accounts, such as Keoghs or IRAs.

A partial list of HSA custodians is below. As new custodians are announced you will find them on www.HSAfinder.com.

Definitions

Although HSAs are for medical expenses, they use some language you might be more used to hearing in the area of retirement savings.
Contribution: A deposit; any money you (or your employer, if you have an employer-sponsored HSA) put into your account.
Distribution: A withdrawal. Whenever you use your HSA to reimburse yourself for qualifying medical expenses, you're taking a distribution from your account.
Return: Growth in your account not related to deposits, such as increases from interest.

Can You Be Your Own Custodian?

The law specifically prevents a business from simply opening up a banking arm to offer HSA accounts. You can't set up a financial wing for the purpose of taking in deposits from employees and administering their accounts.

This part of the law was written to prevent companies from "commingling" their employees' health savings with other assets. It's a big improvement on how big companies have handled Flexible Spending Accounts — employers could take back any money left in the account at the end of the year and add it to their assets. The law also looks to prevent the kind of abuses that have cropped up when organizations mismanage their own pension funds for employee retirement.

One of the best things about HSA accounts is that the money belongs to the employee. It is portable and he or she can take the money with them when they leave the company. There is no "vesting"" — and hence no reason for a business to dabble around with the savings of the worker.

Definition
Vesting is a common provision of employer-sponsored pension, savings, and stock plans. Simply put, it means you must stay in your job for a certain amount of time before you have a right to full benefits under the plan. For example, after five years with the same company, you might vest in its pension plan — earning the right to a retirement benefit. HSAs have no such requirement. The money in an HSA is *always* all yours, regardless of time worked at the company or your reasons for leaving.

Like Fortis, other big health insurance companies are putting partnerships in place to offer you new places to start an HSA that meet the federal requirements. They will compete with every financial institution now offering retirement accounts. Wells Fargo, JP MorganChase, Mellon Bank, and others should all have account products available by the end of the year.

If you're not comfortable in this league, even your current neighborhood savings bank, for example, can become a custodian of your HSA account if it chooses to register with the IRS to handle this as a business service.

So, then, how do you pick the right custodian for your money?

WHAT TO LOOK FOR

FDIC Insurance — a Must

The minimum requirement for the company you choose is that the deposits you make into your account are insured, through the Federal Deposit Insurance Corporation, or FDIC.

Under current law, this national insurance program protects deposits up to $100,000 per account.

Are you old enough to remember the savings and loan scandal of the 1980s? This was a federal debacle, as the U.S. government, using your tax dollars, had to "make good" the deposits people and businesses had put into banks that then went bankrupt. It was a big hit to the American economy — costing hundreds of billions of dollars — but it established forever the value of the FDIC program. Depositors insured by the federal government against default, even people whose banks had gone bankrupt, were able to recover their life savings.

Don't trust your HSA to any institution without FDIC insurance!

All established banks operating in the U.S. offer FDIC insurance on cash deposits, to the extent of the law. Financial companies (like Fidelity and Schwab's) that provide investment vehicles for IRAs and 401(k) plans often make a distinction between investment instruments that are FDIC-insured (such as money market accounts) and those that do not have this protection (stock funds and brokerage accounts).

If you want to protect your retirement savings, don't put your HSA dollars into any account that is not FDIC-insured.

A Track Record

A few national firms have a good track record in handling Medical Savings Accounts and Archer MSAs, because they participated in the pilot programs set up as early as 1997. They may not be household names, but they've been around.

HSA Bank (now a part of Webster Bank) is just one example. American Health Value, a subsidiary of Home Federal Savings, is another.

Even if you don't go with these institutions, it is worth your time to visit their websites (www.hsabank.com and www.americanhealthvalue.com) and examine the offerings. You'll get the benefit of their experience in this area, and a better idea of what to ask when you approach another bank or vendor.

State Regulations

State regulations regarding HSA administration only apply to the custodial institutions doing business within that particular state. However, depositors are free to place their HSA accounts in any custodial institution in any state they choose. Check that state's regulations before depositing.

Using an Online Institution

You can put your HSA deposits into any financial institution that is registered with the IRS to serve as a custodian for HSA accounts. This means that if you can't find a bank within your own community, you can choose a bank in another state. Online banking is the way to go.

Online banks must have an actual home somewhere: First HSA, Inc., for example, extends its online empire from its home base in Reading, PA.

Reputable online banks carry FDIC insurance and meet the requirements of regulatory agencies in their home state. As with insurance companies, there are state agencies that monitor compliance and customer service (see your phone book under state listings for the one the applies to you).

Many taxpayers are already used to "virtual banks" that allow them to pay bills online, get cash or make deposits with an electronic card, accept automatic payroll deposits, and generate electronic checks when a physical check is required. As long as the bank is FDIC-insured, your health savings should be safe.

Profile: Hassan

Hassan runs a five-person business that services copiers, though it's rapidly expanding into information technology outsourcing work. They've never had a health plan, but this year — when one employee's untreated cold turned into pneumonia, and left the company short-staffed for a month — Hassan realized it was time to start offering health care. A high-deductible health plan — with a $200 company contribution into each employee's HSA — is the only option he can afford.

After a discussion with the four others, Hassan concludes that they're all so technology-oriented that it would be a mistake to go with an HSA that doesn't offer online banking. That single criterion makes his decision much easier.

They choose an online vendor and Hassan posts a link to it on the company's employee website. One employee, Leslie — who was self-employed until last year, and still has a balance in an MSA — can roll her old account into her new one without ever leaving her desk.

Like most people, Hassan and his employees prefer to research their health care information online, so it makes sense for them to manage their health care spending online as well. They don't have to spend any time on hold with customer service — so they actually have more time to work. Paradoxically, the money Hassan spends on the new plan is *saving* the company money. It's also paying off in goodwill among the employees, who now have an additional reason to stay with the company.

Opening the Account

If simplicity is your goal, the companies that offer combo plans for both high-deductible insurance and HSA financial management will start to look better and better. By all means look at partnered vendors. They may offer economies (like a single administrative fee) attractive to you.

Remember, if a vendor relationship does not work out, anyone can switch. You can find your own HSA custodian, and move your funds. And if that vendor doesn't work out, you can "fire" the vendor and start again. Be sure there are no exit restrictions before commiting to a vendor.

From the Databank: No Need to Rush

IRS Notice 2004-25 provides "transitional relief" for early adopters who secure qualifying high-deductible policies in 2004 but have difficulties locating a suitable trustee or custodian for their health savings account. For calendar year 2004 only, individuals may retroactively reimburse themselves with tax-free dollars for any qualifying medical expense that occurs after the first day their HIGH DEDUCTIBLE policy is in force, but prior to the opening of an actual health savings account. The grace period extends to April 15, 2005, which should allow taxpayers plenty of time to select a suitable custodian.

Source: *IRS Notice 2004-25*, March 30, 2004

IRS Reporting Requirements and Your Privacy

The reporting requirements for HSAs are, again, very similar to the reporting requirements for IRAs and other retirement fund accounts.

1. You, the taxpayer, must report to the IRS the total amount of each year's contribution, interest or dividend income, and all distributions (payments) from your health savings account. (To see where this goes on tax forms, see Chapter 7, "Realizing the Tax Advantages of an HSA.")

2. The bank or custodian will also file a report to the IRS showing the totals of deposits, interest or dividend income, and disbursements (distributions), for the HSA account associated with your Social Security Number. An "IRS Match" (when the IRS compares the information it receives from you with what it receives from your account custodian) determines that the numbers are the same for both reports.

3. If you have an HSA at more than one bank, or are spreading your contributions among different custodians, they will all do reports — and it's your responsibility to make sure your total contribution limit has not been exceeded. (See the Contribution Calculator on page 96)

4. The details of your disbursements are not part of the custodian's report — just the total dollar amounts. When you sign a custodial agreement, you agree to bear responsibility that your disbursements are a "qualifying medical expense" as defined by the IRS. The bank is not responsible for making sure your expenses qualify. (Some credit card companies intend to offer a combined card, with masking programs to keep this personal information from their service representatives who view records or communicate with cardholders.)

5. Detailed information on disbursements (such as doctor addresses or name of drugstore chain) is usually provided to you in the form of online statements and end-of-year summaries or printouts. Under current privacy laws, the bank or custodian may make this information available to the IRS if the IRS requests such information. However, the information the custodian can give is restricted to the date, the identity of the provider, and the amount — not the details of the service or care rendered.

6. People who use HSAs should keep their own detailed records of disbursements, with information on the service or care rendered, in the event the IRS requests a clarification of an expense that may not qualify. You do not need to send receipts to the IRS when you file your taxes.

About the Paperwork

Opening up an HSA is not much different from opening a regular checking account.

An inch-thick stack of forms to fill out can be dismaying, especially if your goal in opening a high-deductible health plan was to get *away* from bureaucracy. But don't panic. On closer inspection, many of these forms should look pretty familiar.

Application Form: You fill out this form with your name, address and Social Security number. You will have to provide a copy of an identifying document, such as a driver's license, state ID card or passport that confirms your existence. Employees (including the self-employed) must also fill in the employer's name, mailing address, and contact information.

Custodial Agreement: This outlines your business agreement with the bank or other custodian. It also outlines your responsibilities regarding IRS reporting of both contributions and disbursements.

Debit Card Application: You'll have to complete a separate form to apply for a debit card with a PIN number. Often, this is a Visa or MasterCard. There are also several independent debit cards being offered that roll all of the functions into one convenient card.

Rollover Form: If you are "rolling over" funds from a different kind of health savings account, such as an MSA, there is another form for this information, which is passed onto the IRS at tax time.

Definition

Rolling over refers to the process of closing one tax-advantaged account and putting the money directly into another such account. A rollover allows you to avoid paying income taxes (and certain penalty taxes) on the balance of the closed account.

Restrictions and deadlines do apply — make sure you're familiar with them before you initiate a rollover.

Beneficiary Form: Because an HSA is an inheritable asset, you will be asked to designate an heir or beneficiary in the event that you die.

Power of Attorney Form: This is the option to allow another person to write checks for you or use a second debit card. It is often called a "third-party" or "power of attorney" authorization.

If you've got a family plan, it makes sense that you and a spouse would both have debit cards in your wallets, and be able to write checks to cover expenses for family care. So your spouse can be the third party. You may also designate a domestic partner, sibling, parent or any other adult as the third party.

It's your call. If you've set up a "single" high-deductible health insurance policy plan, you still might want someone to be able to go out and buy your prescriptions if you are bedridden. True, you could always write that helpful person a check from your HSA account to cover their expenditure. But giving someone else a power of attorney can allow you to get your medical bills paid, and your deductibles met, even if you're in a coma.

HSA CUSTODIAL ACCOUNTS: THE BASICS

- A vendor may be a bank, business, brokerage firm or individual, but must be registered by the IRS and satisfy any other state and federal regulations.

- A vendor should offer flexible options and instruments for depositing, withdrawing, transferring, and investing HSA funds.

- A vendor should provide FDIC insurance to protect the bulk of savings.

- A vendor should facilitate IRS reporting with easy access to account information, and periodic documentation to account holders.

- Account owners, not vendors, are responsible for IRS reporting of contributions and expenditures for qualified or unqualified expenses.

- Vendors may be teamed or partnered to provide a "one-stop shop" for medical and financial services.

Putting The Money In: Who Contributes And How Much?

5

Managing your HSA account is a balancing act. You want to maximize the amount rolled over and accumulated from year to year, and at the same time to be sure you are getting the health care you need for you and your family.

How much money should you place into your HSA?

If you completed a Chapter 2 Worksheet #1, you now have a rough estimate of your out-of-pocket medical costs for the next year. Having read through Chapter 3, you have decided on a deductible limit. You may even have your qualifying high-deductible insurance policy "in force" right now. If you just finished Chapter 4, you have a good idea of what you should look for in a custodial account for your first HSA dollars.

For most, an interest-bearing checking account, with a debit card, will be the "starter" HSA.

Health Savings Account Balance At Age 65
Based On $2,000 Remainder Each Year

Start At	5%	6%	7%
Age 25	$253,679	$328,095	$427,219
Age 35	$139,521	$167,603	$202,146
Age 45	$69,438	$77,985	$87,730
Age 55	$26,413	$27,943	$29,567

Health Savings Account Balance At Age 65
Based On $1,000 Remainder Each Year

Start At	5%	6%	7%
Age 25	$126,840	$164,048	$213,610
Age 35	$69,761	$83,802	$101,073
Age 45	$34,719	$38,993	$43,865
Age 55	$13,207	$13,972	$14,784

There is no minimum contribution to an HSA. You can open most accounts with as little as $100, and your contributions thereafter can be a few dollars per month, if that is all you feel you can put aside. And there are no restrictions on how large the balance can grow as your savings accumulate with interest or dividends.

But there *are* restrictions about how much you can deposit in a single tax year.

Determining Your Contribution Limit (Indexed Annually)

There is a limit to the maximum amount you can contribute into an HSA each year and still get a tax deduction. Generally, it is 100 percent of the deductible for your insurance policy. If you chose a $1,000 single deductible, the most you can contribute to an HSA in any tax year is $1,000.

But a further cap applies. If you purchase a $3,000 individual insurance policy, your contribution maximum for the year, as an individual, is $2,650 (in 2005). If you chose the highest family deductible allowed in the program ($10,000) you may only contribute, and take as a tax deduction, up to $5,250 (in 2005). If you are fifty-five or older, you can put an additional $600 in your account to catch-up in 2005, the annual catch-up amount escalates in future years until 2009 and thereafter.

The contribution limit is also pegged to how many months of the year you qualified for an HSA. The tax deduction for HSAs is pro-rated to the tax year. This means that anyone starting HSAs this year will run into the issue of *partial-year contributions*. If you've only had your qualified high-deductible insurance policy in place since July 2005, your contribution limit for 2005 is automatically cut in half. If you have a $1,000 deductible on your insurance policy, you would only be able to contribute (and deduct from taxes) a total of $500 for the 2005 tax year.

Don't worry about calculating your HSA contribution limit based on partial months. If your coverage began August 10, 15, or even 29, then for HSA purposes you were covered for the whole month of August.

If you enter the program in October 2005, your maximum contribution is restricted to what you can get for three months; on a $1,000 deductible policy, your maximum contribution will be calculated as follows: $1,000 / 12 months = $83.33 x 3 months = $250.

If you start in October, the maximum you can deposit, given this deductible, will be $250 for the 2005 tax year.

THE CONTRIBUTION CALCULATOR

Many of the websites that either offer HSA-qualifying insurance policies or serve as bank custodians for HSA accounts include a "contribution calculator." You can plug in the numbers, click an onscreen button, and get a figure that represents your contribution limit.

The math, however, is easily done with a pencil and paper:
A. Your insurance policy deductible is: $_____

Note: If this number is greater than $2,650 and you have an individual policy, write in $2,650. If this number is greater than $5,250 and you have a family policy, write in only $5,250. (Amount listed is indexed annually.)

B. Divide this amount by 12 (the number of months in a tax year) to get your monthly pro-rated amount:

A $_____ / 12 = $_____

C. Determine how many months your policy is in force, in this tax year: (1–12) _____

D. Multiply the number from "B" by the number from "C." The total represents the maximum amount you may contribute this year:
B $_____ x C $_____ = $_____

Note: For HSAs, a policy is considered "in force" by the IRS on the first day of the month that you receive coverage through the policy. If you sign a policy agreement on July 24, the policy is retroactively in force as of July 1.

The initial cash outlay for the first, partial year will probably be a few hundred dollars at most. It's a fairly painless way to get used to the HSA concept. In later years, you should be able to adjust both your deductible levels and your contribution levels to suit your individual savings needs and health care costs.

Special Rules for Those Over 55

To allow older taxpayers to "catch up," the current law allows HSA participants to stretch their contribution limit by an additional $600 in 2005. This means that if a person over 55 has a $1,000 deductible, his or her legal contribution may be $1,600 for the tax year.

In subsequent years, the extra contribution is indexed and becomes an even larger figure. Under current law, by 2009, the "catch up" amount for those over 55 will be an additional $1,000 per tax year.

These additional amounts must also be pro-rated for partial-year participation, and reduced by 1/12th for each month the individual was not covered by a qualifying high-deductible plan. Stretched out over a full year, the additional monthly contribution for the additional $600 would be $50 per month.

Catching Up on Catch-Up Contributions

Why do we keep saying "catch up"? What are older investors catching up *to?*

Well, younger investors have the luxury of putting money in their HSAs now and letting it grow for years. Investors over age 55 may need to put more of their money in shorter-term investments, which could mean that older investors would see smaller benefits from their HSAs. Instead, the law gives them a leg up by allowing them to make larger contributions — that is, to have more money growing over a shorter period of time.

If you have a 401(k) plan, you may already be familiar with the concept of catch-up contributions. A similar provision began applying to personal retirement savings several years ago, when the government raised the annual 401(k) contribution limit.

Maximizing Your Contribution for the Tax Year

As a real-life example, let's revisit the three workers at the housewares factory discussed in Chapter Two. Each of the three participants opted for different levels of deductible, so Bob, John and Joan all have different contribution limits.

Because the company started the program on April 1, 2005, participants can put up to 75% of their deductible, subject to the cap, into their HSAs. All three of them established an interest-bearing checking account for their HSA, placing $100 each in this "starter" account.

Joan, the shop worker with the $1,000 deductible, can put up to $750 in her account. But she has only put in $100 so far. She has until April 15, 2006, to put in an additional $650 if she wants to. Even if she does wait until the last minute, she will be able to "roll over" that sum into her account for the 2006 tax year, and may deposit an additional $1,000 during 2006

John, the foreman, has the $5,000 deductible family policy. His deductible limit is $3,750, also 75% of his deductible. And because he is 56 years of age, the over-55 rule allows him to contribute an additional $400 for 2005. He has been putting away $90 for each two-week pay period. At the end of the first nine months of the program (19 weeks) he will have deposited and additional $1710. John might still put in more: in fact, he can deposit an additional $2,315 by April 15, 2006 (perhaps by transferring funds from other investments).

Both Joan and John could maximize their HSAs by contributing more in 2004. They may, in fact, wish to use their funds for health care expenses during this first year. Or, if they stay healthy, they may be able to roll over all they've deposited, creating a firm base for next year's HSA investments.

It's Bob, the owner, who may feel the squeeze in his first few years on the program. Bob reported he had also not deposited any more than the initial $100. Yet Bob has a $10,000 deductible family policy, and because of the contribution cap ($5,150 for families) in 2004 he may only contribute up to 75% of that sum, or $3,862.

Bob still has until April 15, 2005, to deposit the additional $3,762 he may legally contribute. And common sense suggests that he should strive to deposit up to his limit, so the amount may be "rolled over" if it unused in 2004, to help him pay for expenses towards his family's larger deductible of $10,000 per year.

Penalties on Excess Contributions

Current law mandates a penalty if you contribute in excess of your limit for the tax year. Even if your employer makes the excess contribution, you will be penalized with a 6 percent excise tax on the entire amount that is over the limit.

The IRS will also treat amounts in excess as income with no offsetting deduction. The tax responsibility will belong to the owner of the account, even if the employer made that excess contribution.

From the databank: The IRS on Excess Contributions

Q-22. What happens when HSA contributions exceed the maximum amount that may be deducted or excluded from gross income in a taxable year?

A-22. Contributions by individuals to an HSA, or if made on behalf of an individual to an HSA, are not deductible to the extent that they exceed the limits {described}. Contributions by an employer to an HSA for an employee are included in the gross income of the employee to the extent that they exceed the limits {described} or if they are made on behalf of an employee who is not an eligible individual. In addition, an excise tax of 6% for each taxable year is imposed on the account beneficiary for excess individual and employer contributions.

However, if the excess contributions for a taxable year and the net income attributable to such excess contributions are paid to the account beneficiary before the last day prescribed by law (including extensions) for filing the account beneficiary's federal income tax return for the taxable year, then the net income attributable to the excess contributions is included in the beneficiary's gross income for the taxable year in which the distribution is received but the excise tax is not imposed on the excess contribution and the distribution of the excess contributions is not taxed.

Source: *IRS Notice 2004-2*

The "guidance" supplied by the IRS in its notice on HSAs (Notice 2004-2) does state that the 6 percent penalty tax will be waived if a distribution of the excess (including the earnings thereon) is made to the account holder in a timely manner. The easiest way to do this is to write an HSA check to yourself, in the amount of the excess, before December 31, of the relevant tax year. The earnings on the excess will be taxable on distribution.

If you can prove the check to yourself is a reimbursement for out-of-pocket qualified medical expenses in the second year, you may not have to pay any tax on that amount. You'll need receipts to back this up, naturally (See Chapter 6 for more on self-reimbursement).

Profile: Elton
Elton, 33, is a self-employed marketing consultant. His wife works part-time in a retail store that doesn't offer health benefits. They have two children, ages 4 and 18 months, and cover the entire family under a high-deductible health plan.

Elton speaks bluntly — which is why his clients hire him — and his opinions on health care are no exception. One way or another, he figures he's going to be paying for most of the care his family needs. "Even if I were working for a big firm," he says, "they'd be jacking up my premiums this year and telling me sorry, but they just couldn't afford to keep covering us."

Make no mistake, he's not crazy about the high-deductible plan either. "I think catastrophic coverage is pretty much worthless," he says, laughing, "unless you have a major emergency." He knocks on wood for good measure. A major emergency, for his family, would be one that left him unable to work, which would force his wife to pick up more hours at the store, which in turn would mean they'd have to pay more for day care for the kids. Elton takes some comfort in knowing that his $8,000 deductible is within the limits of what he could pay for out of his personal savings.

The real value of the HSA, as Elton sees it, is its potential as a savings vehicle. Before the HSA, his only retirement savings plan was a Roth IRA; he contributed the maximum to it, but still knew it wouldn't be enough on its own. He also plans to contribute the maximum to the HSA every year — not because he expects to use it for health care, but because it lets him double his annual retirement savings.

Avoid a Tax Penalty

It's up to you to monitor your HSA contributions and make sure they don't exceed your legal limit. Use the contribution calculator on page 98 and make sure you know what your limit is. Then pay attention. A monthly number-check, at the same time you balance your checkbook, ought to be enough — it will take only an additional minute or two.

If your employer contributes to your HSA, he or she will monitor that amount as well, but it doesn't hurt to check. If you go over the limit, it's your tax responsibility — not your employer's.

If you do go over the contribution limit, don't panic. You may still be able to avoid the penalty tax by using the excess money on a qualifying medical expense.

EMPLOYEE VS. EMPLOYER CONTRIBUTIONS: PROS, CONS AND USEFUL COMPROMISES

Keeping track of contribution limits can get sticky where employers decide to contribute to worker HSA accounts, or when workers arrange to have their own HSA contributions deposited as a payroll deduction. Since both employers and employees may contribute to an HSA, your employer may limit your job-related contributions (payroll deductions or non-wage compensation).

Reportability

Only employer contributions to HSAs are reportable to the IRS. Your employer is not responsible for making sure that contributions remain within the caps and limits stipulated by the law, even if the boss or the business makes the contribution. You are responsible for making sure that all deposits during the course of the tax year are under the limit. Remember that your limit varies based on your situation — it depends on your deductible and, if you obtained qualifying coverage this year, how many months you've been covered.

The Non-Discrimination Rule

The amount of money your employer may deposit into your HSA is subject to the non-discrimination rule. Under this rule, if any one employee (including the boss) is given money from the business as a contribution into an HSA, every worker with a participating HSA must also receive a contribution for his or her HSAs.

Small-business owners should read Appendix B to learn more about complying with the non-discrimination rule.

It does not have to be exactly the same amount, but it must be a "comparable" amount. The rule makes it illegal, for example, for a business with a salaried owner to place $5,000 from company funds into his or her HSA, claim the expense as a business tax deduction, and then give each of ten employees only a $50 HSA contribution for the same tax year. The IRS says this is not "comparable." It is not fair. However, it is up to the IRS to enforce the rules.

The Portability Factor

A big difference between HSAs and other types of work-supported health care plans is that HSAs are completely portable. Employees can take the money with them when they go. By law, employer contributions do not "vest" — you can't delay HSA contributions for six months or a year with a new employee, as you may if you sponsor a 401(k) plan.

Example: The Hat Store

John runs a hat store and hires Bob and Jill to work as hat sellers. As a sole proprietor, John decides to obtain a high-deductible ($2,000) insurance policy for himself and opens an HSA account. He puts $500 into his HSA account, and writes off both the cost of his insurance policy premiums, and the $500, as deductions from his personal income tax.

The next year, John decides to offer a high-deductible insurance policy to his two salaried workers. Bob is already covered by his wife's full-benefits insurance policy so he says no. Jill has no other health insurance, so she agrees to sign on for a high-deductible policy ($2,000) as well.

John pays the premiums for Jill's policy and takes that cost as a tax-deductible business expense.

Jill also opens an HSA account. She puts $200 of her own money into it. John contributes $500 to his own HSA plan, and each deducts that sum from their personal income tax.

Jill has what she perceives as a valuable job benefit: John, the hat store owner, is paying for her health insurance premiums. He is also putting $500 into her HSA account — if for no other reason than he wishes to put $500 in his own HSA, and expects to write off the total contribution of $1,000 as a deductible business expense for that tax year.

But John, the owner, cannot be sure that Jill will quit as soon as he puts $500 into her HSA account. So maybe he won't do it so fast, or all at once.

As the current law is set up, John has the option to *pro-rate* that $500 over the year. He can divide that $500 into 12 months, and deposit $42 per month (or $19 for each two-week pay period) into Jill's HSA account.

If he wishes, he can set up a similar payroll plan for himself, and deposit $19 every two weeks into his own HSA account.

If Jill quits the job (or he has to fire her) before the end of the tax year, he does not have to continue to contribute to her HSA. She has ceased to become his employee. He may, however, continue to contribute biweekly to his own account. When the next April 15 rolls around, he may be able to contribute an additional $500 (to the limit of his $1,000 deductible) to his own account. He can still legitimately deduct the second $500 as a business deduction. And because he no longer has any employees with a comparable plan, he no longer has to worry about the non-discrimination rule.

As for Jill, since her HSA is "portable," she will be able to fund it herself, as long as she maintains a qualifying high-deductible health insurance plan. Even if she uses the money in her HSA to fund continuation of this HIGH DEDUCTIBLE plan through COBRA, John no longer has any obligation to add another dollar to her HSA.

HSA CONTRIBUTIONS: THE BASICS

Contributions are currently capped* at $2,650 per year for individuals and $5,250 for families. (If you have a family, but you are covered under an individual high-deductible health plan, you may contribute to your HSA only up to the individual limit.)

Contribution amounts are further limited by the size of your deductible and how many months of the year your policy has been in force.

Contributions made by your employer are not tax-deductible for you.

Money your employer deposits into your HSA account is subject to the non-descrimination rule.

You or your employer may make one or more deposits at any time.

Those 55 years or older can make extra "catch-up" contributions to their accounts; the amount allowed in 2005 is $600.

Current year deposits may be made until April 15 of the following year.

* 2005 amount, indexed annually

Taking The Money Out: How to "Spend" HSA Funds

6

HSA money must be used for qualified medical expenses to remain tax-free. This chapter helps you make the most out of your HSA expenditures.

You can make tax-free withdrawals from your HSA account to pay for "qualified medical expenses" as soon as your account is activated and if you have an opening balance. This is the money you can use to pay your medical bills, until you reach the annual deductible limit for your health insurance policy plan.

What's a Qualifying Medical Expense?

The IRS definition of "qualifying medical expenses" is broader than most insurance companies', and you can use your HSA to pay for many things your health insurance won't cover:
- Laser eye surgery
- Over-the-counter medication (provided a doctor prescribes it)
- Glasses and contact lenses
- Treatment for substance abuse
A more detailed list appears later in this chapter, but regulations do change. You can always find the most up-to-date list of qualifying expenses online, either at this book's companion website (www.hsafinder.com) or in Publication 502 on the IRS website (www.irs.gov).

If retirement savings is your goal, you do not have to make any withdrawals from your HSA during the course of the year. If you're healthy enough, you won't have to spend many of those tax-free dollars, and can aim to maintain a high account balance — and save most of the account for retirement.

Sicker people will wind up with less money in their accounts at the end of the tax year, and will have lower account balances once they reach retirement age. Many will start the HSA program because they anticipate using tax-free dollars to pay for *expected health care expenses* that relate to an existing ailment, injury, or course of treatment. And healthier individuals will use HSAs to save additional retirement funds, especially if they're already contributing up to the limit of their IRAs or Keoghs. (Remember that an HSA is not a primary retirement savings vehicle. Your HSA can augment your retirement savings quite handsomely, but it shouldn't be the only way you save.)

Sticker Shock: Adjusting to Pay-as-You-Go Health Care

When you first begin self-managing your health care costs, you may be shocked to discover just how much medical costs in America have spiraled out of control. A routine checkup from your family pediatrician may cost $175 for an office visit. A prescription for a brand-name drug to control your cholesterol may cost $600 for a month's supply. The sicker you are, the more it costs. One chemotherapy treatment at New York's Beth Israel Hospital costs $14,000.

Many of us have been shielded from the true costs of health care. This is one of the reasons health care costs have risen faster than inflation, especially over the last five years — it's a lot easier to spend money thoughtlessly when you don't know the true value of what you're buying. If you had health care coverage through an HMO, for example, that pediatrician's fee was only $25, as far as you knew: $25 was your co-pay. Your insurance plan picked up the other $150 and paid the rest of the doctor's fee.

A by-product of this masked approach to health care costs, as we discussed in the introduction, has been the soaring costs of health insurance premiums. In fact, a plan with a co-pay only seems like the better deal until you figure in what you've paid for your HMO insurance premiums. Let's say you pay $450 per month for your share of an employer-based health insurance policy plan.

In one month, you take your child to the pediatrician once. You pay $25 for the office co-pay. Your health insurance costs for the month: $475.

How would it work if you had a less expensive high-deductible insurance policy that qualified you for an HSA? Such a policy might cost you $300 per month for family coverage.

In one month, you take your child to the pediatrician once. You pay $175 for the doctor's fee — the entire price of the visit. Your health insurance costs for the month: $475.

You're paying the same amount. It only appears to be different. You probably hardly notice the $450 you pay for premiums, because it's deducted automatically, payday by payday, since the day you agreed to have your share of the premiums "taken out of your pay." The only figure you really give attention to is the $25 on the check you write from your personal checking account. It seems small, and manageable.

Under a high-deductible health plan, care does seem more expensive — at first. Remember that your premiums are far lower than they would be under an HMO. And your HSA entitles you to realize tax savings on a number of health-related expenses you might not otherwise qualify to deduct.

For those conditioned to the myth of co-pays, writing a check for $175 may seem all wrong. The figure looks bigger, and it could be significant if you wrote the check on your personal checking account.

But under the HSA program, you can write that check from your HSA instead. If you've followed the instructions in Chapter 5, there should be enough in the account to cover a $175 check for the doctor. If you have been depositing money in pro-rated amounts each month or with every paycheck, your HSA funds have been accumulating fairly painlessly as well.

If your medical costs have been high in the past, paying the bills with tax-free HSA dollars may be perhaps the least expensive way to meet the deductible on your health insurance policy. When you meet the deductible limit, the plan pays for all further health care costs for the year, as long as your qualifying high-deductible health insurance policy is in force.

Profile: Anna
Anna, an administrative assistant, is 46. Her husband Mike covers her and their three children under the PPO offered by his employer. That

strategy was working just fine for them until Henry, their youngest child, started showing signs of autism. The diagnosis was confirmed last year, just after Henry's second birthday.

In just over a year, the family's medical expenses have tripled. Occupational therapy could help Henry, and Mike's PPO covers a certain number of visits, but it's less than half the number that doctors recommend. In the past, when cash was tight, Anna would volunteer to stay late at work — picking up other assistants' extra work and earning overtime. But her company, like so many others, is tightening its budget, and it's worked out a complicated work-balance plan in the administrative pool that has all but eliminated overtime hours.

Anna and Mike know they'll have to spend a lot of money on Henry's care, but helping him is not optional. When Anna learns that occupational therapy is a qualifying expense under HSAs, the choice is clear. She'll cover herself under an individual high-deductible health plan, and contribute the maximum to an HSA, knowing that most of that money will go towards Henry's therapy.

Anna's and Mike's combined income is around $55,000 a year, so the HSA strategy also works out in their favor at tax time: it puts them in a lower tax bracket. They avoid tax altogether on the $2,500 Anna has put in the HSA,

A Breakthrough: Who Is Covered?

At first glance, it may seem that you can only use your HSA dollars to cover medical expenses for yourself if you have an individual plan. And you may think that if you have a family coverage plan, you can only use your HSA dollars on medical care for the people named in your plan as family members.

But guess what? The insurance company doesn't make the rules about how your HSA dollars can be spent. The IRS makes the rules. And according to the IRS, you can spend your HSA dollars on anyone that you claim as a spouse or dependent on your personal income tax. As long as you spend the money on what the IRS terms a qualifying medical expense, your withdrawals on behalf of dependents remain tax-free.

This means that you can pay for your sister's long-term care expenses with your HSA dollars, even if you only have an individual deductible plan for yourself — provided that your sister is named as a dependent on your Form 1040 tax return. It also means you can write HSA checks for a spouse's or child's co-pays, if your spouse or child is covered by a traditional PPO or HMO health plan.

If you list someone as a dependent on your tax forms, you can use your HSA funds to pay for that person's health care expenses tax-free — *even if he or she isn't covered under your high-deductible health plan.* Yes, really.

The IRS had confirmed its support for the qualification of expenses for dependents as follows:

Distributions from an HSA used exclusively to pay for qualified medical expenses of the account beneficiary, his or her spouse, or dependents are excludable from gross income. In general, amounts in an HSA can be used for qualified medical expense and will be excludable from gross income even if the individual is not currently eligible for contributions to the HSA. (Source: IRS Notice 2004-2)

Where Co-Pays Are Covered: The Exceptional Exception

Example: Trudy and Jack are married and file taxes jointly, claiming children Karen and Kenny as their dependents. Jack works for a large corporation and has a family insurance policy through his employer. The policy is an HMO that only covers Jack, Karen, and Kenny. If Jack, Karen or Kenny goes to the doctor, there is a $20 co-pay for each office visit.

Trudy runs a catering business from their dining room. She is covered by her own individual high-deductible insurance policy with a $2,500 deductible. Each year she deposits $2,500 into her HSA account.

Question: Can Trudy write checks from her HSA to cover the $20 co-pay each time her husband or her children see a doctor?

Answer: Yes, because everyone in the family unit is represented in the family's joint tax return. It does not matter that Trudy's insurance policy is an HSA-qualifying policy with no co-pays. The IRS makes the rules, and under current rules any payments of any size to a doctor may be a "qualifying medical expense."

Bear in mind that Trudy must pay the full price for her own doctor visits, because no co-pays are allowed with her HSA-qualified policy plan. This means she may pay $150 or more when she sees her own doctor.

Sticker shock is probably not an issue with Trudy. Everyone in her family is covered by an appropriate insurance plan, and most of the family's out-of-pocket medical expenses can be paid for with tax-free dollars, from Trudy's HSA.

The self-employed may be less prone to sticker shock regarding the cost of care under a high-deductible health plan. For the self-employed, health care has been expensive for a long time. The surprise may be that now they can actually save some money!

Payment Mechanisms

Typically, when you open an HSA account you receive a checkbook with about 25 checks, plus a debit card. Some account custodians charge you for the checks (anywhere from $10 to $25) and will charge you for additional check orders as well.

Besides debit cards and checks, other payment vehicles permitted by the new law include certain types of credit cards issued by the custodian and stored-value cards in specific dollar amounts. Stored-value cards for HSAs are similar to store gift cards or phone cards. The starting balance is debited every time the card is used, until the amount is used up.

For practical purposes most HSA holders will use the checks to pay for doctor office visits and large-ticket items. They'll use a debit card for pharmacy prescriptions and to purchase over-the-counter medicines: even a bottle of aspirin is considered a qualified medical expense under the IRS rules for HSAs, if your doctor gave you a prescription for aspirin.

Common-Sense Limits

Staying within the limits of qualified expenses with your debit card is a matter of common sense. An HSA debit card cannot be used as if it were a debit card from your checking account: you can't purchase prescriptions, some aspirin on sale for the medicine cabinet, a pack of gum and a bottle of shampoo, and still expect to get the benefits of lower-cost health care.

The IRS is not going to watch over your every purchase with the debit card. But the IRS will expect you to stay within contribution limits. Whether you can deposit your maximum contribution each year, or you can only put aside a few dollars per month, it makes no sense to use up dollars you may need later for a true medical expense.

What's Deductible and Considered a Qualifying Medical Expense?

The IRS makes a distinction between "qualifying" and "unqualifying" expenses for HSAs. In tax parlance these withdrawals are referred to as either qualified or unqualified distributions — the opposite of contributions, which represent deposits to the account.

Only distributions provable as qualifying medical expenses will be tax-free. Unqualifying distributions are considered to be "income" for your tax year and will be subject to both federal and state income taxes, as well as an additional penalty tax of 10 percent of the amount that was spent.

The IRS has created some pretty clear guidelines, and a good list, of what it considers qualifying medical expenses. This appears in IRS Publication 502, "Medical and Dental Expenses." The publication is available for free from the IRS, and is downloadable as a PDF from www.irs.gov. It is often reproduced in materials handed out by insurance vendors who sell HSA-qualifying high-deductible insurance policies.

Look Familiar?

If you've had a health care flexible spending account through your employer, you probably already know what expenses you can pay for with your new HSA — the guidelines are exactly the same.

IRS Qualifying Medical Expenses

Abortion
Acupuncture
Alcoholism Treatment
Ambulance
Artificial Limb or Prosthesis
Artificial Teeth
Bandages
Birth Control Pills
Braille Books and Magazines
Breast Reconstruction Surgery
 (post-mastectomy only)
Capital Expenses *
Car Modifications (for disabilities)
Chiropractor
Christian Science Practitioner
COBRA Payments
Contact Lenses & Solutions
Crutches
Dental Treatment
Diagnostic Devices (i.e. blood
Sugar test kits for diabetics)
Drug Addiction Treatment
Eyeglasses
Eye Examinations
Eye Surgery
Fertility Enhancement (some
treatments excluded)
Guide Dog or Guide Animal
Hearing Aids
Hospital Service
Laboratory Fees
Laser Eye Surgery
Lead Paint Removal In Home
Learning Disability
Legal Fees (with restrictions)
Lodging (treatment-related only,
 with restrictions)
Long-term Care Insurance
Long-term Care (Some)
Meals (treatment related, with
restrictions)

Medical Conference Fees (relating
to chronic illness; no lodging or meals)
Medical Information Plan
Medicare Parts A and B
Medicines (prescribed)
Mileage (14 cents per mile)
Nursing Home
Nursing Services
Operations
Optometrist
Organ Donors
Osteopath
Oxygen
Psychiatric Care (including costs
for residential care)
Psychoanalysis
Psychologist
Special Education
Sterilization
Stop-Smoking Programs
Surgery
Telephone or Television modifications
(for disability)
Therapy (not specified)
Transplants
Transportation (treatment related)
Trips (for treatment)
Tuition (special education only)
Vasectomy
Vision Correction
Weight-loss programs (prescribed)
Weight-loss foods (only if prescribed)
Wheelchair (or maintenance)
Wigs
X-Rays

*Deductions for capital improve-
ments to make homes handicapped
accessible depend on resale value of
your home before and after the modifications.

Figure 6-1   Source: *IRS Publication 502*

This is the list of qualifying distributions as this book goes to press. Because the list may change over time, updated lists are also available online, at www.irs.gov, and on the website created for this book, www.HSAfinder.com.

As you can see, the list of medical expenses that qualify under current IRS rules is much broader in scope than what has been traditionally covered by health insurers. So broad, in fact, that someone with a $1,000 deductible insurance policy might easily reach the deductible limit in a single week.

Professional care that qualifies includes medical doctors, dentists, optometrists, nursing services, and emergency care.
Other types of health care providers that also qualify include:
> Christian Science Practitioners
> Chiropractors
> Psychiatrists
> Psychologists
> Acupuncturists (but not herbalists)
> Therapists (certain certifications may be required)

Treatments not often covered by health insurance are included:
> Alcoholism or drug addiction treatment
> Fertility enhancement
> Laser eye surgery
> Prescribed weight-loss programs
> Stop-smoking programs
> Special schools and homes for the mentally retarded

Medical equipment, appliances and other personal items also qualify very generously:
> Artificial limbs and prosthetics
> Dentures and other artificial teeth
> Contact lenses
> Eyeglasses
> Braille books and magazines
> Crutches and wheelchairs
> Hearing aids
> Guide dogs and other helper animals
> Birth control pills

Perhaps the most extensive area of qualifying expenses includes costs that may be incurred when seeking treatment. These include trips and travel exclusively for the purpose of a treatment, as well as meals and lodging associated with such trips.

Qualifying treatment-related expenses may include:
> Telephone or television modifications for disability
> Legal fees related to treatments
> Medical conferences (must be related to a condition)

What Does NOT Qualify?

Anything that may possibly be considered "cosmetic surgery" will not qualify as a medical expense under the HSA program (unless the surgery is related to a medical condition, as in the case of a birth defect or a mastectomy). Similarly, non-medical out-of-pocket expenses that arise from a medical event — such as the birth of a healthy baby — may not qualify. Hospital fees? No problem. Diapers? Problem.

EXPENSES NOT COVERED UNDER HSAs
> Cosmetic surgery
> Teeth whitening
> Maternity clothes
> Diaper services
> Health club dues
> Electrolysis for hair removal
> Hair transplants
> Household help or babysitting*
> Marijuana for glaucoma (or other controlled substances)
> Nonprescription drugs and medicines
> Food supplements not prescribed by a doctor (e.g.Ensure TM.)
> Over-the-counter vitamins or diet drinks (e.g., Slimfast)
> Swimming lessons
> Weight-loss programs not prescribed
> Funeral expenses

* You may still be able to take a tax deduction for these expenses, or even pay for them tax-free if your employer offers a dependent care flexible spending account. The Dependent Care Tax Credit could also help you. See IRS publication 503 for more information.

What's Debatable?

Some borderline expenses remain on the table and must wait for further guidance in the form of future IRS notices about HSAs.

For example, if you hire a firm to remove lead-based paint from your new home or apartment, the IRS will consider this a qualifying expense. But if you need to build a wheelchair ramp for grandma when she comes to visit, that may not be an expense that qualifies.

You'll always find the most up-to-date guidelines online, at www.HSAfinder.com or www.irs.gov.

Over-the-Counter Confusion

One of the biggest new myths surrounding HSAs is that any over-the-counter pill or salve you might buy at a drugstore is a "qualified medical expense."

This is absolutely not true. The law provides that these small items, such as aspirin, sunscreen, vitamins, "aromatherapy" candles, acne creams, Epsom salts and Ace bandages, qualify *only* if they have been *prescribed*.

In other words, if your chiropractor or dentist suggests you buy some aspirin on the way home, to ease the ache from your treatment, *ask for the recommendation in writing*.

Paying for common home remedies with HSA funds is not going to be a money saver, if you figure in the expense of the doctor visit to get the prescription for an over-the-counter decongestant or a bar of acne soap.

Smart HSA holders will continue to pay for cheap drugstore items out of their own pockets or pocketbooks — not with their HSA debit cards.

Choosing Your Own Doctors, and Meeting Your Deductibles

As we discussed in Chapter 3, traditional HMOs and PPOs (the kind that don't qualify for HSAs) discourage people from using doctors or services not included in their "network" of providers. If you want to go to a different doctor, you pay the entire fee yourself, and often the amount cannot be applied to your deductible. If you had a Flexible Spending Account (FSA), you could use those funds to pay the doctor's fee.

Qualifying high-deductible plans for HSAs that are straightforward indemnity policies generally will let you apply *any* doctor's fee that is a *qualified medical expense* to your deductible. HSA-qualifying high-deductible PPOs might not allow you to apply the fee for your out-of-network doctor to the deductible; however, you may still be able to apply it to your total out-of-pocket cost cap for your insurance plan.

Getting the PPO Discount

If your qualifying high-deductible plan is a PPO, it's smart to use providers within your network. Instead of a co-pay, there may be a substantial reduction in the doctor's fee, often a discount of 25-30 percent.

Some insurance vendors make you and the doctor go through a billing procedure; this verifies the discount, and you get a bill later from the doctor that reflects the discounted fee. Other vendors may give you an insurance card that says "no co-pays" but also serves as a discount card when you pay at the desk. Some vendors give you a separate discount card good for lower-priced prescriptions at certain pharmacy chains.

Take the In-Network Advantage

You will reach your deductible faster if you have many doctor bills. But because the insurer would prefer you not reach your deductible so soon, they'll gladly cut your costs to slow you down. One way they do this is to pre-negotiate discounts with providers in the network. That's why using a "preferred provider" generally costs you less.

The IRS will consider most doctor fees and doctor-prescribed medicine as a qualifying medical expense. If you choose to reimburse yourself for such an expense, you don't pay tax on this "distribution" from your HSA. Theoretically, you could travel to Tahiti and pay for a Shaman's healing ceremony with shells and leaves — as long as you could convince the IRS that this was a qualifying medical expense.

Bottom line: While HSA contribution limits for a single tax year are determined by your deductible limit for in-network services with a PPO, **the IRS sets no dollar limit on how much of the HSA you may spend in any year, as long as the distribution is a qualifying medical expense.**

As a practical matter, the amount of money that you spend depends upon the balance in your account. While deposits during the first years may be small, accumulated savings can provide a cushion of tax-free dollars over time.

For extremely severe medical conditions — such as those requiring organ transplants — many insurers rely on specialized providers, often called "Centers of Excellence." These providers have special experience or facilities for certain procedures — designed to raise the quality and efficiency of your care. When an insurance plan relies on such centers, the plan may cover your travel expenses. Even if your plan doesn't cover these expenses, your HSA will allow you to pay for them tax-free.

Becoming a Better Health Care Consumer

HSAs were designed to help people save money to pay for unexpected medical bills. The combination of high deductibles and tax advantages really does encourage people to save more and make more cost-effective choices when they are spending their own money on health care.

The early adopter of a high-deductible insurance policy and an HSA account might be tempted to spend up the deductible limit as quickly as possible. One physical, dental and vision checkups, a new set of dental X-rays, and a dozen boxes of disposable contact lenses — you might be well on your way to reaching a $1,500 deductible in your first week. Then, you might safely coast through the rest of year, relying on your policy to cover all other anticipated or unforeseen medical costs.

Two Examples

Jackson lives in California, and has a favorite "pain-free" dentist he's been going to for years. Jackson moves to New Mexico, and signs up for an HSA-qualifying high-deductible PPO plan through his new employer. This plan does not include dental care. He also opens an HSA account. Six months later, he has pain in his upper jaw. His California dentist, naturally, isn't on the "provider list" — that list only includes oral surgeons who work in New Mexico.

Question: Can Jackson visit his California dentist and pay for the visit with HSA funds? Does it count towards his deductible? Can he deduct his plane fare as well?

Answer: The PPO will probably count the California dentist's fee towards Jackson's deductible, but not the plane fare. The IRS will qualify the dentist's fee, but may not consider the plane ticket a qualifying medical expense. Why? Because Jackson theoretically could find a comparable dentist in the state where he now resides. If Jackson pays for the plane ticket with HSA dollars, the expense might be taxable as an income distribution.

Susie and her family are covered under a qualifying high-deductible PPO with a $3,000 deductible. She has opened an HSA. Susie's daughter has a rare medical condition. The best specialist for this condition is three states away, and not a member of the PPO's network.

Question: Can Susie take her child to the specialist and pay for the visit with HSA funds? Does the travel count towards her deductible? Can she deduct travel expenses, including several overnight hotel stays, and restaurant meals as a further qualifying expense?

Answer: Susie's PPO may or may not include the specialist's fee and the travel expenses to her deductible, but it may apply the fee amount to her out-of-pocket maximum. According to IRS guidelines for HSAs, the specialist's visit, lodging and meals are all qualifying medical expenses.

In Control Again

Debbie's employer (a major national corporation) just began offering a "consumer-based" health plan with an HSA. Debbie, 44 and married with no children, was one of the first employees to switch over.

"I actually think the responsibility is one of the best aspects of the plan," she says. "It gives a sense of control and feels much less bureaucratic, since nobody is telling you what providers you can see."

Surveys by insurance giant Aetna indicate that many people are discovering they prefer to manage their own care rather than let "managed care" plans do it for them. Interestingly enough, these people may do a better job of managing their care too. Early findings on the "consumer-driven" model of health care show that people in these plans tend to seek more preventive care *and* spend less overall on health care than do their counterparts in managed care plans.

Of course, given the choice, we all just want to be able to take care of ourselves. Consumerism, HSAs and other changes in the health care industry may just make it easier to do that.

The drawback, of course, is the contribution limit, which is determined by your deductible (in a PPO the limit is determined by your deductible for in-network costs). If you put $1,500 in your HSA, spend it all in a week on qualifying expenses, you can still take that $1,500 off your gross taxable income. But now you can't put any more money in for the rest of that tax year. And you have nothing saved for the future.

What will happen the next year? What if business is slow? In your new benefit year, you'll still need to pay up to your $1,500 deductible for continued health care. But you may not be able to afford to put as much as $1,500 into your HSA for the new year.

What happens if you get sick in the new year? Really sick? You don't have $1,500 in your HSA account — your balance is zero. And you may not have that much in your personal checking account. You're stuck back where you were before HSAs — paying your medical bills with after-tax dollars in the second year.

Don't Spend It All in One Place!

There's no rule that keeps you from using up your entire HSA at any time. But that doesn't make it a great idea! If you use up your HSA — You're missing out on income from the invested account balance. You might leave yourself without a financial safety net in case of a medical emergency, either now or in retirement.

If you're used to an employer-sponsored flexible spending account — where the goal is to spend the whole account before the end of the year so you don't have to forfeit the balance — you may need to adjust your way of thinking about these funds. Once you've adjusted, you'll probably find it pleasant: no more use-it-or-lose-it pressure!

Now you can see how the HSA program is really meant for you to save, not spend, your health care dollars. If you had left a balance of $500 in your HSA account the first year, you'd be able to withdraw that money right now, immediately, right now when you need it.

This is the short-term example of how HSAs can provide an ongoing cushion for your medical expenses. The long-term benefits are just as concrete.

The Rollover

Let's say you managed to deposit $1,500 into your HSA for the first year, spent less, and had a balance of $1,000 at the end of the tax year. You can still take the entire $1,500 as a deduction from your gross income tax. But your account balance is now $1,000.

In the second year, even if business is bad, and even if you get really sick, you still have that $1,000. It is immediately accessible to pay for medical bills, even if you'll be well on the way to meeting your $1,500 deductible limit for your second benefit year.

The Power of Interest

There's one undeniable advantage to starting an HSA this year: Your money has longer to grow. Check out Chapter One and Five for an illustration of the difference compound interest can make over time.

What happens if business is good? What if you manage to save $1,000 each year in your HSA account?

Compound interest is what happens. If you kept your HSA in an interest-bearing checking account paying 2.75 % interest, in five years your HSA will have accumulated $5,367 — enough to pay your year-ly out-of-pocket deductible three times. In the intervening years, you've never had to worry too much about unexpected medical expens-es; you've always had sufficient money in your HSA to pay out any amount up to your deductible limit. Your distributions have been running just under $500 each year, and you're still taking the entire $1,500 off your taxes.

If you've maintained a $1,000 balance of contributions for ten years, you have well over $11,000 in your HSA. It's a modest sum. Your balance might be higher if you moved some of the money into a high-er-yield account. (At 7% interest, the balance would be closer to $15,000.)

If, at the end of ten years, you are no longer insured — or on a differ-ent type of health plan, or on Medicare — you can still use the $15,000 to pay for qualified medical expenses. Plus, you got a 50 per-cent return on your thousand-dollar-per-year investment, over ten years, and it's still all tax-free. And if your HSA contributions helped you edge into a lower tax bracket, you may have saved thousands of additional dollars in taxes on the rest of your income.

As described in Chapter 4, you may set up more than one HSA account to spread your savings through a variety of investment vehi-cles to gain interest and dividends. There is no penalty for "rolling over" or transferring funds from one HSA account to another, and any gains from good investing are also tax-free.

Using HSAs to Buy Other Forms of Insurance

Other innovations in the HSA program fall into place as an additional cushion in case of hard times. For example, if you become unemployed, you can use the money in your HSA to pay premiums on a COBRA and retain your former employer's health insurance for at least 18 months.

Similar innovations recognize the need that lifestyle needs change over time. For example, if at the end of ten years, you reach the age of 65 and are hired by a large corporation that offers you only an HMO policy plan, you can use the funds accumulated in your HSA to pay for your share of the premiums for this employer-sponsored health insurance or for a separate retirement insurance plan.

If your family high-deductible policy covers a spouse or other dependent who is eligible for Medicare, payments for Medicare Part A and Part B are also considered to be qualifying medical expenses by the IRS. However, premiums for a Medicare supplemental insurance policy (such as Medigap) do not qualify under the current law.

HSAs cannot be used to pay for the premiums on your high-deductible insurance policy, or for someone else's HMO policy premium.

You may pay for these types of insurance through your HSA:
- Premiums for dental or vision care insurance.
- Premiums for COBRA continuation coverage when you leave a job.
- Premiums for temporary insurance coverage while receiving
    unemployment benefits.
- Premiums for qualified long-term-care insurance policies.
- Premiums for Medicare Part A or Part B and Medicare HMO.

Financial Cushion? Or Money Mattress?

In the event of severe financial difficulties, money saved in an HSA account may be immediately withdrawn to meet a crisis. All you have to do is write yourself a check. It is true that you will have to report this "distribution" as potentially taxable income, as you would if you "cashed out" your IRA or Keogh. But you don't have to withdraw the entire amount, just what's really needed for this important, non-medical need.

This is yet another reason why HSAs are truly "the better rainy day fund."

Hardship Withdrawals

You may withdraw funds from your HSA to avert a financial crisis. Examples include:
- To avoid eviction from or foreclosure on your primary residence
- To pay for secondary education for yourself or a dependent.
If your expense does not fall within these definitions, your distribution will be taxable as income.

Five Good Reasons to Hold On to Your HSA Dollars

1. Savings can be instantly accessible for emergency expenses.
2. Savings can be used to meet deductible limits in hard times.
3. Savings can be used to pay COBRA premiums to continue coverage offered by a former employer, for at least 18 months.
4. Savings can be invested for retirement or anticipated job or lifestyle changes.
5. Savings can be used to pay an older spouse's supplemental insurance policy premiums if he or she becomes eligible for Medicare before you.

Testing, Testing

Under transitional relief rules, some of the better HSA-qualified high-deductible policy plans may waive fees for routine preventative care regardless of your deductible, and you won't have to pay any fees for an annual physical, children's immunizations, and certain cancer screenings. Otherwise, most of us can expect to use some of the HSA dollars to pay for occasional medical care — and it may be wise to use these tax-free dollars to pay for annual checkups, dental or vision exams, and similar types of preventive care. Depending on your family history, other screenings, such as mammograms or colonoscopies, may make sense to you.

You may want to research conditions, treatments and tests before you decide to request a laboratory test. Many websites — such as webmd.com, your insurance company's site, or sites devoted to specific conditions (additional websites are listed on Page 201) — can direct you to the information you need to make your decision.

But you may find out that you no longer care to have extensive medical tests done to probe a condition in more detail, now that you're paying for such tests with your own tax-free dollars. If you bumped your head, do you really need a brain scan? If your son is allergic to your cat, is finding out that he's also allergic to dust mites worth the expense of a battery of patch tests?

Everyone's medical needs are different. Under the old system, which tests or treatments you took usually depended on which ones were reimbursable under your insurance plan. With HSAs, you have more choice, but the downside is that you may not be able to afford every test or treatment you want to try.

From the Databank: Self-Managed Care at Aetna

Workers who "self-manage" health care spending accounts are more likely to be pro-active when it comes to preventive medicine, according to a research report by Aetna's head of product development, Robin Downey.

The analysis studied 13,800 Aetna employees who opted for a model-spending plan (a version of an HRA plan) in 2003, switching from enrollment in traditional plans in 2002. Among this group, office visits for routine physicals, including gynecological exams, increased by 30.1 percent. Employees who switched also had fewer emergency room and outpatient visits, compared to a control group who stuck with an HMO or PPO option. The study also showed that 51 percent of the employees had money left over in their health care spending accounts at the end of the year.

Source: Reported in *AIS News*, March 2, 2004.

Long-Term Care (LTD)

The following material was researched and provided by John O'Leary, long considered a leader in this area.

What might happen if I develop a need for long term care?
Most people don't want to think about the possibility that they might need long term care at some point in their lives. It's a difficult prospect to consider, so people put off thinking about it, often until it's too late. A better approach is to consider that long term care may be a very real possibility, and start planning now for how to pay for it.

What is the "right" age to start thinking about LTC insurance?
The biggest problem is that people wait too long to think about buying LTC insurance. Premiums are lower at younger ages, and because premiums are designed to stay level throughout the policy "locking in" premiums at young ages is a good strategy. Mid 30s is not too early, particularly if the plan is offered by your employer.

Where would I feel comfortable getting care?
Most people say that they want to stay home as long as possible to receive long term care. In part that's because of the negative images conjured up by nursing homes. There are, however, other appealing options, and more are emerging all the time. Think about where you would like to receive care, and what places you would avoid. If you plan now you can have those choices when the time comes.

Can I reasonable afford to pay for care from my savings and other assets?
Many people think they can fund long term care from their savings. But it's worth "doing the numbers" before you come to that conclusion. Take a look at what the nursing home costs per year are in your area today. Recognize that long term care costs are going up 5-8% per year, so factor is 2-3 times the current number for inflation. The average length of stay in a Nursing Home is about three years, and most people use home care services for a year or two prior to that, so figure 5 years for the typical duration of care.

A sample calculation would look something like this: $50,000 per year (the national nursing home average) doubled for inflation x 5 years of care = $500,000 in potential long term care expenses.
While this may seem like a lot, it is actually on the low side of what a long term care scenario would look like 10, 15 or 20 years from now. Can you, or do you want to reserve a half million dollars or more from

your savings and assets to pay for long term care? My view of a reasonable range for LTC expenses, depending on where they live and their age is $250,000 on the low side to $1 million on the high side. The million high side number is not the absolute max someone could spend, but its probably the highest number anyone should reasonably plan for.

Assuming I decide long term care insurance can help me, what should I look for in a long term care policy?
Everyone is different, with differing needs and risk tolerances. So keeping that in mind, here is one man's opinion on what to think about when buying an LTC policy.
* "Buy flexibility" wherever you can afford it.
    - Select a plan that pays for more than just basic nursing home care. Make sure the plan covers assisted living and adult day facilities, home care, and if possible "informal care" which includes features like housekeeping services. Also look for plans that have "alternative plan of care" options which may pay for emergency monitoring systems and home improvements to help you receive care at home.
    - Most plans today have a "total pool" of benefit dollars that is subject to daily or monthly limits. You want the highest amount of flexibility in the way you use the total pool so pick the highest daily or monthly limits you can afford. When you receive benefits, you don't have to use your entire daily limit, but the flexibility is there if you need it.
    - Be willing to pay more for monthly limits, as opposed to daily or weekly ones. This a more flexible approach, particularly for homecare.
* Be careful of overbuying.
    - Some people view long term care insurance as a way to fund as much of their potential long term care expense as possible. This approach is very expensive. Features like unlimited lifetime maximums and built-in inflation, while appealing, drive up premiums. I recommend avoiding them.
    - In reality, most people are better off just trying to offset some of the costs they would otherwise have to fund on their own. Pick a lifetime maximum (total pool of dollars) that represents the amount of assets/savings you want to protect, and pick a periodic inflation option that gives you opportunities to increase your protection if you want and can afford to (make sure there are no limits to the number of times you pass on the inflation opportunity when offered without going back through medical underwriting).
    - Avoid extras like lapse protection (sometimes called a non-

forfeiture benefit). While the concept of getting at least some benefit for the premium you have paid in is a good one, the relatively small benefits most of these provide often don't justify the required increased premium.

* Take heed of reputation and experience

Make sure you select a company that will stand behind its promise to you, many years in the future, is probably the most important LTC choice you can make. Buy a household name ideally with some LTC insurance experience and strong ratings. LTC insurance is still relatively new, but several of the key players have strong names, excellent ratings, and enough LTC experience to know what they are doing. Companies that I would suggest are Hancock, MetLife and Prudential on the group side and Genworth, NY Life, Northwestern along with Hancock on the individual LTC side.

Keeping Track and Correcting Mistakes

Oh no — you used your HSA debit card or wrote a check from your HSA account to pay for something that did not qualify as a medical expense.

Can you correct this mistake, or will you pay a penalty instead?

Your HSA custodian is required to report all distributions from your HSA account to the IRS. You get a copy of the report from your custodian vendor at the end of the year. It's up to you to tell the IRS how much of the distribution total was for qualifying medical expenses, and what part of the total does not qualify.

What you must do is include the unqualified amount in your taxable income for the year. The qualified amount is noted on a special form (See Chapter 7 for more on reporting to the IRS). If you've been careful, the error may be just a small amount that does not significantly affect your tax bill.

A Tip on Cautious Spending

Nobody wants to carry around IRS Publication 502 everywhere. If you're not certain whether an expense counts as qualified, *don't* use your HSA debit card to pay for it. Use your credit card or regular checking account. Later, if it turns out the expense does qualify, you can reimburse yourself from the HSA.

In the coming land rush to HSAs, the potential for fraud and scams is great. Generally you should not take anyone's word on whether a treatment, medicine, or device will qualify in the eyes of the IRS. Refer to the IRS's own lists, and if you have any doubt, seek the advice of a competent tax professional.

One way to handle expenses in the gray areas is to pay for these with your personal accounts, not your HSA account. If you later determine the expense will qualify, you can write yourself a check from your HSA account to reimburse yourself. The IRS will allow this as long as you can provide relevant receipts as proof of your out-of-pocket expense. You may wish to photocopy the check you wrote to yourself, staple the

---

Nine Ways to Get the Most Out of Your HSA Dollars

1. Use network providers as often as possible if your policy is a PPO.
2. Ask out-of-network providers to discount their services because you will pay their fee immediately (with an HSA checkbook).
3. Negotiate a discount for series of treatments (such as psychiatric or chiropractic services) if you pay them up front for a series of five or ten sessions (again, with your HSA checkbook).
4. Ask that your prescriptions be for generic or over-the-counter medicines wherever this is possible. If your insurance plan includes a formulary — a list of discounted (or "preferred") brand-name drugs — adhere to it as much as you can.
5. Shop around town for the best prices on prescription products, as prices can vary from $10–$20 from one pharmacy to the next.
6. Use a discount card, if your health insurer has provided one, when you purchase prescription items.
7. Use the debit card, if your HSA custodian has provided one, only for prescription medications and supplies.
8. Don't stint on preventive care. Annual checkups (including dental and vision care and cancer screenings when appropriate) for you or your family can catch small problems before they become big ones.
9. Don't pass up useful free services. Many communities offer free mammograms or blood screening services, asthma or diabetes management, weight-loss programs, or stop-smoking clinics. Your employer or local hospital may have a health fair to promote disease prevention or screen for treatable conditions. Take advantage of it!

receipts or the bill to the copy, and file it until tax time.

Keep a file for all medical receipts, in case the IRS requests more information about any of your distributions. You do not have to file any medical or care-related receipts with your tax forms.

SPENDING YOUR ACCOUNT: THE BASICS

- Qualified expenses are only those listed under IRS Code Section 213 (d) expenses, and include:
  Over-the-counter drugs
  Prescription drugs
  Doctor visits, labs, x-ray and other diagnostic and treatment services.

- Qualified expenses are only those expenses to used to pay for the health care needs of HSA account holders and their dependents, provided that those dependents are named on the account holder's tax return.

- HSA funds may be not be used to pay for insurance premiums, except for certain exceptions.

- Non-qualifying withdrawals are taxable as income — at your normal income tax rate — plus a 10 percent penalty.

- Non-qualifying withdrawals are taxable, but no withdrawal penalty applies for Medicare-eligible beneficiaries, or upon disability or death of the account holder.

- Account holders must keep adequate records on expenditures.

Realizing the Tax Advantages of an HSA

7

We've mentioned the tax advantages associated with HSAs throughout this book. This chapter explores these options more fully and provides a roadmap to help you comply with the tax-advantage regulations, and get the most out of them as well.

Some people call HSAs "Medical IRAs." To some extent this is true from a tax perspective. In addition to an above-the-line deduction from income for contributions, the exciting feature of HSAs is that they let you withdraw money at any time for qualified medical purposes without a tax penalty. The funds and any earnings (e.g., interest or dividends) they may accumulate over time are *never* taxed, even after age 65, if the money is used directly for qualified medical expenses. As with IRAs, the money is yours. You decide how much to contribute and you own the account even if you change jobs or stop working.

This Chapter discusses how and where to deduct HSA contributions on your personal income tax return. If you're self-employed, you may want to skip ahead to page 136, where you'll learn how and where to deduct HSA-related expenses as a legitimate business tax deduction. *(Unless otherwise noted, this discussion relates to federal tax matters only. The IRS is issuing new rules on a regular basis for clarification. As of publication, states determining taxable income by reference to federal rules are expected to adopt HSA rules as well, but some rules will differ by state.)*

TAX EXEMPTION AND TAX DEFERRALS FOR INDIVIDUALS

On your personal income tax return, the amount of your HSA contribution should ideally equal the limit of your allowable deduction under your insurance plan. To make up any difference, the current law allows you to make contributions into an HSA as late as April 15 for the previous tax year. Use the Contribution Calculator (see Chapter 5, page 98) to determine the maximum amount you can contribute and still get the tax advantage. Try not to put in any more if you can help it. As explained in Chapter 5, contributions in excess of the limits wind up includable in your gross income, and may be subject to a 6 percent excise tax as well.

Why Contribute Between January 1 and April 15?

Let's say you're self-employed, and last year was rather lean. Though you have a $2,000 deductible, you only managed to contribute $800 to your HSA. But in the early part of this year, things turn around. You're getting new clients and you're busier than you ever dreamed you'd be. The April 15 rule lets you take advantage of your new productivity: you can contribute up to $1,200 for *last* year — plus the $2,000 for this year — and get a tax break on $3,200 of this year's income.

All eligible contributions into an individual or family health savings account, as of January 1, 2004, are exempted from personal income tax. They are **tax-free for that tax year**. It does not matter if you don't spend all the money in your HSA for pressing medical expenses over the course of the year. As long as the money went into a qualified HSA, you can still take the tax deduction for the full amount of the contribution.

More importantly, whatever leftover money is in the account may be accumulated until age 65, when it may be taken out — as you need it. After age 65, if any of the money is used for medical expenses, it remains tax-exempt. If the money is used for something else besides a medical expense, it will be taxed at the then applicable rates but without penalty. Typically, if you are retired, you will have less income and pay a lower tax rate. But the distribution doesn't get taxed until the year it is withdrawn (distributed) from the account.

Thus, distributions that are not totally tax-free may be **tax-deferred.**

Another incentive to wait until you're 65 to spend your HSA funds: If you're retired or semiretired, you're likely to be in a lower income tax bracket than you are now. So even though you'll pay income tax on the distributions, it may be lower than what you pay now.

Tax Treatment of Earnings

Earnings (including interest and dividends) accumulated in an HSA account are tax-free for the tax year they occur, and also tax-deferred until withdrawn for purposes other than payment of qualified medical expenses.

Withdrawal Penalties

Withdrawal penalties are fully explained in Chapter Six. Remember that many medical expenses covered in the HSA program are not eligible in other programs. Read the lists of covered medical expenses carefully, and don't assume that an expense is not covered without checking with IRS materials or your tax advisor.

Avoid a Penalty!
Check www.HSAfinder.com or www.irs.gov for the most up-to-date lists of qualifying expenses.

Death Benefits

The money saved in an HSA is considered an "inheritable asset" subject to estate tax. Taxes may be paid by your heirs or assigns in the year the funds are released from your estate, at the same rate as other inherited, previously untaxed income. Under the current law, the entire amount may pass to a surviving spouse without estate tax.

Definition
An **assign** (also sometimes called an assignee) is a person or entity who receives some or all of a benefit that would otherwise go to you. Common assigns are former spouses and creditors.

Tax Rule on Rollovers

You can roll over accumulated funds from an Archer MSA or other HSAs into your current HSA custodial account, without paying a tax or penalty. Rollovers are not subject to contribution limits; but you do not get an additional deduction for them in the current tax year. In other words, if you started an HSA in 2006 and put $500 into it, and then take $10,000 you had previously stash away in an MSA, and "roll it over" to add it to the HSA, you can deduct the $500 as an AGI adjustment — but not the $10,000. That's because you've already taken a tax deduction on the rollover — in the year you first saved it.

Example: Don

Don, 35, single, and in good health, rarely spends his HSA dollars. He finds the cost of health insurance "abusively high," so he thinks any tax deduction is a step in the right direction.

A lifelong independent contractor, he's never been eligible for an employer-provided pension or 401(k) — and "now that all these pension plans are collapsing," he says, "that's starting to seem like it was a wise choice." When he heard about HSAs, he signed up as quickly as he could; the savings potential just made sense.

He's not thrilled with his current HSA vendor, which charges a monthly fee. Once he finds a bank he likes, he'll start contributing the maximum annual deposit allowable. In conjunction with his IRA, this will allow him to set aside around $8,000 every year.

If you participated in a Flexible Spending Account (FSA) this tax year, pending legislation may allow you to roll over as much as $500 from that account into an HSA for the next tax year.

Under current law, rollovers from an IRA, HRA, or other health reimbursement plan from an employer or a flexible spending arrangement, are not allowed without a penalty. In other words, you cannot empty your IRA and put the money into your HSA directly. If you decide to empty your IRA, it will be considered a distribution, counted as a part of your taxable income for the year, and subject to a penalty under the IRS rules for early withdrawal.

How Big Is the Early Withdrawal Penalty?
For most people, it's 10%. That may not sound like much, but remember that your early withdrawal is also subject to regular income tax. So if you empty an IRA of $60,000 before age 59? and you're in the 25% tax bracket, you'll forfeit a whopping $21,000 in taxes — over a third of the account's value. It *really* pays to leave the money in the account.

For the majority of people opening an HSA this year, the tax advantages of an HSA will not outweigh the tax penalties incurred by moving money out of an IRA. For many types of HRAs and FSAs, the point is moot: unused funds channel back to the employer and are not "portable" to the employee.

Rules for Reporting Premium Costs and HSA Contributions

Contributions into an HSA can be made either by an individual or by an employer. If the individual makes the contribution, the amount is DEDUCTIBLE from the individual's TOTAL INCOME (Line 22 on the current version (2004) of Form 1040).

If your employer makes a contribution, the amount is EXCLUDABLE from your WAGES (Line 7 on the current version (2004) of Form 1040). The excluded amount is supposed to be noted on the employee's W-2 paperwork, but you should check to make sure your wage figure, which is minus your employer's contribution, is correct on your W-2, so you can enter a correct amount on Line 7 on the Form 1040.

If an employer paid for all of your high-deductible insurance premiums, only that employer is entitled to deduct this sum as a business expense. If you paid part of the premium out of your salary, your costs for the premium will be noted on the W-2, but this sum is not excludable from your wages.

Self-employed sole proprietors deduct their premiums on the Form 1040, not on the Form SE. If you're self-employed, you may deduct 100% of these costs.

TAX STRATEGY: If Your Spouse Works in the Business

This strategy is so smart we wish we thought it up. But we didn't:

> ...*Think about how you could maximize your deduction for your family's medical care by hiring your spouse. Let's say you are self-employed and do not have health care coverage. You hire your spouse as your only employee. Let's assume there is no question about the bona fide employer-employee relationship between you and your spouse. Your spouse receives from you compensation for services he or she performs (which is deductible on your Schedule C) and includes the compensation as gross income on your jointly filed tax return. (This is a wash — it does not change your Adjusted Gross Income.) You also adopt a written employer-provided accident and health plan that, by its terms, covers all employees of your business. During the year, you reimburse your spouse under the plan for medical expenses incurred on behalf of the spouse, his or her spouse (which is you), and their dependents (which are your kids). You deduct the medical reimbursements to your spouse on Schedule C as a business expense under Section 162. By doing this you completely avoid the 7.5 percent of AGI {Adjusted Gross Income} reduction on Schedule A.*
>
> *Do you think the IRS would go along with this? No problem. In a recent advice memorandum sharing the same facts, the IRS ruled that the amounts paid . . .were deductible as a business expense under Section 162.*
>
> — *Page 192,* JK Lasser's Taxes Made Easy for Your Home-Based Business *(Fifth Edition) John Wiley and Sons, Hoboken, NJ* ©2003

Here's how this strategy works with an HSA: The insurance policy taken out by your spouse is a high-deductible family insurance policy. The policy premiums are paid for by the business, deductible as a business expense on your Schedule C.

But now, instead of reimbursing your spouse-employee each time an expense is incurred, you — the employer-spouse — place an amount of money in your spouse-employee's HSA, up to the allowable contribution limit. You could do this at the start of the year, or wait until the end of the year (or as late as April 15 of the next year) and merely contribute an amount that equals a reimbursement — again up to the contribution limit of the deductible.

If you have other employees with HSA accounts, the business will also have to make a "comparable" contribution to them, under the non-discrimination rule (see Chapter 5 and Appendix B). But if your only full-time employee is your spouse, the point is moot.

A note: As of this writing the IRS does not allow this advantage to other relatives or to domestic partners, even if they have been "legally married" in their state.

Rule of Thumb: Reporting to the IRS

If your employer made a contribution to your HSA, you don't get the tax adjustment for that specific amount. Instead, your employer gets to claim that specific amount and deduct it as a business expense.

If you're running a business and designate yourself, family members, or others as employees, see "Setting Up Your Payrolls for HSAs" in Appendix A for IRS reporting requirements.

HSAs and the Form 1040 ("U.S. Individual Tax Return")

The amount of money you place into your HSA for the 2004 tax year is, under current law, excludable from your gross income. This exclusion should help lower your individual income tax.

For 2004, the IRS on Form 1040 has established Line 28 for reporting your "Health Savings Account Deduction." This is in the section for "Adjustments to Gross Income."

As with the Archer MSAs, a rundown of your contributions and disbursements may be noted on a separate schedule, Form 8889, for your 2004 tax return.

Remember, under current law you have until April 15 of the following year to deposit contributions into the account for that previous tax year.

An additional note: For calendar year 2005, an HSA established by an eligible individual on or before April 15, 2006, may pay or reimburse on a tax-free basis an otherwise qualified medical expense if the qualified medical expense was incurred on or after the later of:

(1) January 1, 2005, or
(2) the first day of the first month that the individual became an eligible individual.
The general rule that states, *"The qualified medical expenses must be incurred only after the HSA has been established,"* continues to apply to HSAs established for calendar year 2006 and later years.

IF YOU'RE SELF-EMPLOYED: FINDING BUSINESS DEDUCTIONS IN THE TAX CODE

The basic rules for tax deductions for businesses are found in Section 162 of the Internal Revenue Code (otherwise known as the IRC) enacted in 1986. Most years, amendments are made to the IRC code and the tax deductions available for business expenses change a little. In 2004, some changes have been made to accommodate HSAs, and other existing rules, such as rules for deducting the costs of health insurance premiums for workers, have been modified.

Tax Exemption and Business Expense Deductions for the Self-Employed

If you are running any sort of business you are familiar already with the main tax filing forms used for a sole proprietorship. They are the Schedule C or C-EZ ("Profit or Loss From Business") and the Schedule SE ("Self Employment Tax").

As a sole proprietor, you are required to pay self-employment tax on the profits from your business. The ONLY amount that is taxed is your net business profit after business-related deductions — this is Line 31 on your Schedule C, and Line 2 on your Schedule SE in 2004.

You also have to pay income tax on it when you add the profits to your Gross Income, which you do when you ink that figure into Line 12 on the 1040. In effect, you are double-taxed.

If you have no employees and you file a form SE, you may not be able to make an HSA-related business expense deduction. However, if you hired a tax accountant or benefits planner to help you figure out your HSA strategy, you may be able to deduct those fees under "Legal and Professional Services" (Part II, Line 17).

If you're self-employed and a sole proprietor, you cannot write off your health insurance premiums as a business expense. You get the tax

> Self-Employment Tax Rates for 2004 (for net earnings exceeding $400)
> - Tax on net earnings (i.e., profit) from self-employment is 15.3 percent.
> - 12.4 percent goes to Social Security, and 2.9 percent for Medicare.
> - The maximum amount of net earnings that may be taxed for Social Security has increased to $87,900.
> - All net earnings from self-employment are subject to Medicare's 2.9 percent tax.

break on your Form 1040, when it's time to "adjust your Gross Income." As of 2004, you may deduct 100 percent of the premium fees, if you are self-employed, from your gross income. The cost of your high-deductible insurance premiums — the entire cost — gets deducted as an "adjustment." In 2004, you put this expense on Line 28 in the "AGI" section.

If you're self-employed, you'll be able to see a tax advantage from an HSA. The question is how you record it. Depending on your circumstances, it may be an adjustment to personal gross income, or a business expense.

Your deduction for your contributions into your own HSA account, as noted above, is another adjustment in the AGI section that benefits everyone who starts the HSA program this tax year.

Sole Proprietors with Employees

This is where HSAs truly begin to shine. Here is how to make them tax shelters for your personal income, and for your business, at the same time. You can use this strategy if you only have two employees — and even if one of them is you, and the other your spouse or minor child.

Let's say you are earning $70,000 from your business profits this year. You're looking around to see how much of your $70,000 earnings you can shelter, so you can pay less personal income tax on it.

Small businesses with 20 or fewer employees could reap impressive tax savings from HSAs — right away.

If you are eligible to contribute $5,000 to an HSA this year, only $65,000 of your personal income will be taxable. If you are in a 30 percent tax bracket, you'll pay $1,500 less in income tax this year.

In past years, you'd use your IRA or Keogh as the personal tax shelter. But the amount you could shelter was limited. With earnings of $70,000, you can still only put $3,000 into an IRA; that's the maximum amount that would be tax-exempt for 2004 (assuming compliance with rules denying the benefit to active participants in other qualified plans).

This year you can still contribute to your IRA, or try something a little bit different. Or you can contribute to both plans to shelter $8,000 in tax-free income.

Now, let's imagine you've been earning $65,000 in these past years. Business has been good. You are going to earn an additional $5,000 this year. The big difference is that you're not going to spend that $5,000 on a trip to Bermuda. You're going to put that $5,000 into an HSA, to start the health savings account you may need when you retire.

You still get the $70,000. But your taxable income is only going to be $65,000.

Congratulations! You've just rewarded yourself with $5,000. Double-tax free this year. Bermuda can wait, right?

If profits permit, and your company is small enough — say three or four employees — everyone with an HSA might be able to put away the maximum amount (up to $5,850 for family plus catch-up provision) as a tax-free "raise" this year.

If your company has more than 20 employees, however, that may be impractical. The nondiscrimination rule still applies to all eligible employees (see Chapter 5 and Appendix B). If you have helped your employees set up HSAs in conjunction with a high-deductible insurance policy plan, you will, in theory, also have to pony up $5,000 per employee, to satisfy the "comparability" part of the nondiscrimination rule, if you contribute $5,000 to your own HSA.

In practice, you might only contribute $100 to each employee's HSA. And then you'll have to restrict yourself to a $100 contribution (or a larger but "comparable" sum) to satisfy the rule. (See the Example for John's Hat Store in Chapter 5).

If you have 50 employees with HSAs, this is a $5,000 expense. It is also a legitimate $5,000 business deduction. You get to make the call.

Administrative Tax Credit

Administrative costs for setting up an HSA can be deducted as a business expense if your business has fewer than 100 employees. Your business is also eligible for a tax credit of up to $500 for setting up a new retirement plan for your employees. But this amount must be deducted from the administrative costs of the plan — so you lose that equal sum as a business expense.

Where It Goes on the Schedule C

If you're sole proprietorship paying wages to anyone (including yourself), you can include payments made into your HSA and all other employee HSAs as "wages" (Part II, Line 26). The payments are legitimate business expenses that do not qualify as taxable income. If your sole proprietorship pays wages to anyone, see the section on payroll basics in Appendix A.

Rules for Unincorporated Partnerships

Like sole proprietorships, the IRS does not consider unincorporated partnerships taxable entities. But if you have a partner or partners in business, the partnership must file a return to the IRS that reports its income and loss (Form 1065) and each partner's participation in that income, and that loss (Schedule K-1). The information on form K-1 will be reported on each partner's Form 1040 (Schedules E, SE and Line 17 in 2004).

Partners cannot deduct the cost of their insurance premiums as a business expense, but each partner may deduct 100 percent of the premiums he or she has paid on the Form 1040 as a gross income "adjustment."

Example: Tax Consequences for the Design Team

Remember Barbara, Bernice and Cathy from Chapter Two? It's possible that in the first year of business the Design Team won't see any profit. The three women partners will split their losses, and each will be able to deduct the loss from her 1040. Even Cathy, who has a full time income from her other corporate job, can use the loss she writes on Line 17 as an adjustment to offset her other income. She will pay less income tax and self-employment tax. Each partner will be required to file the necessary additional forms with her return (including Schedules E and SE).

If the business sees a profit, the two partners with high-deductible insurance coverage established under the business will be able to deduct the premium payments as an adjustment to gross income (not as a business expense, because this is an unincorporated partnership). Because Barbara and Bernice have also opened individual HSAs, each may deduct the contribution amount from their gross incomes, up to the allowable limit. Cathy cannot.

Therefore, if all three women split the profits and each takes $3,400 as a share:

	Barbara	Bernice	Cathy
Premium payments:	$2,400	$2,400	0 (corporate HMO)
HSA contribution:	$ 500	$1,000	0 (not eligible)
Total AGI deduction:	$2,900	$3,400	0
Taxable Income from the partnership	$ 600	0	$3,400

Cathy has to pay taxes on her share of the profits, which must be included in her individual tax return as non-wage income. Barbara will pay $520 in self-employment tax on $3,400 but will be liable for income tax on only $600. Bernice pays self-employment tax of the same amount ($520) but no income tax on her share of the profits from the business. Cathy pays the same self-employment tax ($520) and is fully taxable for income tax purposes on the entire amount of $3,400 — her share of the profits.

*Note: The deduction for health insurance premiums is only permitted as long as it meets but does not exceed your net earned income from business, and is permitted only for months in the tax year you were not covered by an employer's policy or were covered by a spouse's employer-administered policy. Payment for *a COBRA plan for part of the tax year is deductible because it is considered a form of self-employed health insurance.*

LLCs (Limited Liability Corporations) and LLPs (Limited Liability Partnerships)

Small organizations often operate as an LLC. Under the current tax laws, single-owner LLCs are taxed as if they were sole proprietorships. LLCs with multiple owners get the same tax treatment as a partnership unless they elect to be treated as a corporation. LLPs get the same tax treatment as a partnership. Thus, there are no special tax advantages for LLCs or LLPs under the HSA program.

C and S Corporations

With a "regular" or C Corporation, your business must pay its own income tax on the taxable profits of your corporation. The tax rate for corporations varies by a few percentage points from what is due from married or single taxpayers. Personal service corporations (doctors, lawyers, engineers, architects, etc.) are taxed at a flat rate of 35 percent of their net profit for the year.

If you pay yourself a salary from a C corporation, your health insurance premium costs are a business deduction for the corporation. If you're drawing a salary from the income that derives from your corporate business, you have to pay a personal income tax on that income. After-salary profits are taxed to the corporation. Upon eventual distribution of the profits you pay tax again — the dreaded "double tax" on the distributed profits on your personal tax return.

Double Tax?
Is the government unfair to the self-employed? Not really. In pretty much every setup, the employee has to pay 7.5 percent of his or her income in FICA taxes, and the employer must kick in a matching amount. The "double tax" comes in when employee and employer are the same person.

Tax rules for a "special" or S Corporation are similar to those for a partnership, i.e., you pay tax on your salary and your share of after-salary profits. If your shareholding in an S Corporation is more than 2 percent, you are eligible to deduct the cost of company-paid health insurance premiums as a gross income adjustment on the Form 1040. Other shareholders are treated as employees in the manner of C Corporations.

Incorporated?
See the Appendices, "More Guidelines for Small Businesses," for a corporate tax schedule, a strategic look at when and how to establish HSAs for your employees, and a checklist for setting up payroll. You can also find tools to help your business pick the right employee HSA at this book's companion website, www.HSAfinder.com.

You can see that corporations reporting taxable income (profits) of less than $100,000 qualify for a significantly lower corporate tax rate. Many small corporations therefore strive to find as many business deductions as possible, to get under the $100,000 limit.

HSAs are a new way to get there. Because owner salaries and compensation are deductible as a corporate business expense, contributions into an HSA can cut both the corporate tax and income tax at the same time.

Review the section on Sole Proprietorships to see if you might be able to give yourself a "raise" of up to the maximum contribution that covers your first year's contribution to your HSA. Small corporations and personal service corporations may see the most advantage. So if you work at a corporation with more than 50 employees, your employers may be slow to implement an HSA program, because they may not see an immediate advantage. That doesn't mean you can't open an HSA on your own, if you're covered by a qualifying high-deductible health plan.

Working With the W-2

Each employee gets a W-2 by January 31 for the previous tax year. Copies of each employee's form are also sent to the IRS in early February, along with a summary sheet, the Transmittal of Wage And Tax Statements, also known as IRS Form W-3. Employees who leave your company before the tax year is over may also request a copy of their W-2 earlier, so they can see what the total taxes were relating to their employment.

a Control number	22222	OMB No. 1545-0008		
b Employer identification number			1 Wages, tips, other compensation	2 Federal income tax withheld
c Employer's name, address, and ZIP code			3 Social security wages	4 Social security tax withheld
			5 Medicare wages and tips	6 Medicare tax withheld
			7 Social security tips	8 Allocated tips
d Employee's social security number			9 Advance EIC payment	10 Dependent care benefits
e Employee's first name and initial Last name			11 Nonqualified plans	12a
			13 Statutory employee / Retirement plan / Third-party sick pay	12b
			14 Other	12c
				12d
f Employee's address and ZIP code				
15 State Employer's state ID number	16 State wages, tips, etc.	17 State income tax	18 Local wages, tips, etc.	19 Local income tax	20 Locality name

Form **W-2** Wage and Tax Statement   **2004**   Department of the Treasury—Internal Revenue Service

Form W-2 Reference Guide for Box 12 Codes (See box 12 instructions for information.)

A Uncollected social security or RRTA tax on tips
B Uncollected Medicare tax on tips
C Taxable cost of group-term life insurance over $50,000
D Elective deferrals to a section 401(k) cash or deferred arrangement (including a SIMPLE 401(k) arrangement)
E Elective deferrals under a section 403(b) salary reduction agreement
F Elective deferrals under a section 408(k)(6) salary reduction SEP

G Elective deferrals and employer contributions (including nonelective deferrals) to a section 457(b) deferred compensation plan (state and local government and tax-exempt employers)
H Elective deferrals to a section 501(c)(18)(D) tax-exempt organization plan
J Nontaxable sick pay
K 20% excise tax on excess golden parachute payments
L Substantiated employee business expense reimbursements (Federal rate)
M Uncollected social security or RRTA tax on taxable cost of group-term life insurance over $50,000 (for former employees)

N Uncollected Medicare tax on taxable cost of group-term life insurance over $50,000 (for former employees)
P Excludable moving expense reimbursements paid directly to employee
R Employer contributions to an Archer MSA
S Employee salary reduction contributions under a section 408(p) SIMPLE
T Adoption benefits
V Income from exercise of nonstatutory stock option(s)
W Employer contributions to an employee's Health Savings Account (HSA)

Figure 7-1   Source: www.IRS.Gov, IRS, 2004

The illustration below shows what the W-2 form looks like for the 2004 Tax Year. It is larger and arranged slightly differently from previous forms. Sections a-f identifies the employee by name address, and Social Security Number. (The "control number" is an option for employers who keep track of many workers by employee number).

Wages (plus tips and compensation) for each employee are totaled for the year in Box 1. The amount of wages subject to Social Security (the first $87,900 of wages) goes into Box 3. The amount of wages subject to Medicare tax (everything after the first $400) goes into Box 5.

The amount of withholding for each tax (Box 2, 4, 6) should equal the amount you've already paid in monthly and quarterly installments. For how to calculate withholding, see IRS publication #15-T.

Not everyone will use Boxes 7-11. These report Social Security paid on tips and gratuities, hardship advances for those who will qualify for the Earned Income Tax Credit (EIC).

"Dependent Care Benefits" related to Flexible spending accounts; note the amount the company has invested into an employee's FSA or cafeteria plan. (For more on FSAs, see IRS Publication #15-B).

CONTRIBUTION TAX RULES: THE BASICS

Account holders, family members, or employers may make contributions to an individual's HSA; no contributions can be made by anyone eligible for Medicare.

Contributions made by account holders or family members are tax-deductible ONLY by the account holder (i.e., taxpayer).

Contributions made by an employer are only deductible by the employer; account holders take no deduction on their own tax forms.

An individual or an employer may make one or more deposit(s) at any time throughout the year. Contributions by employers may be pro-rated.

Current year contribution deposits may be made until April 15 of the following year.

Employer contributions must be noted on the worker's W-2 tax form.

Funds in an HSA can be invested, and interest and investment earnings on contributions are not taxable.

Integrating HSAs With IRAs, KEOGHs, 401(k) Plans, SEPs and Health Payment Plans

8

It's estimated that by 2006, 20 million Americans will have Health Savings Accounts, and will view them as a natural extension of prior retirement savings plans that give them tax advantages. In fact, in a study of 6,300 small firms by *Small Business Digest*, almost 23% companies indicating they planned to initiate or offer HSAs in 2005 said they already utilized Individual Retirement Accounts (IRAs), 401(k) plans, or both.

Contributions to a qualified IRA or Keogh save you on taxes twice: they can be deducted as a business expense; and they are not taxed until you take out the money upon your retirement. *If you run a small business, remember that contributions made on behalf of your employees may also be deducted as a business expense.*

If you plan to treat your HSA like a "second" retirement account, you should align your contribution strategy with any existing retirement savings plans. In fact, you may decide to put some money earmarked for some other retirement vehicles — such as under-performing Keoghs or 401(k)s — into the HSA, if it looks like you'll get more of a tax advantage.

Another Plus

There's an additional bonus to tax-advantaged retirement savings accounts: When you do begin to withdraw that money, you may be in a lower tax bracket. So though you do eventually pay income taxes on the money in your account, they may be lower than they would have been in the year when you actually earned that money.

At present, money you've *already* invested in a SEP, Keogh or IRA can't be "rolled over" into an HSA, or be cashed as a source of funds without steep tax penalties. To get the most tax benefits, your long-term strategy should balance your pre-tax contributions between these old and new retirement savings options.

INTEGRATING HSAs WITH OTHER BENEFITS

If you're self-employed, you may already have a Roth IRA, a Keogh or other retirement plan in place. If you have employees, you're probably encouraging them to invest in retirement plan vehicles for themselves.

Should you do more? A lot of smaller companies don't offer pensions or retirement plans. Many grumbling bosses look at the payroll deductions for Social Security, FICA, FUTA, and worker's comp for each employee and send in the required monthly withholding payments with gritted teeth. They think they are paying enough already. They may simply not have enough cash flow to offer an additional retirement benefit — their own survival over the decades to come may be an open question!

If you would like to do more, that's great. But you don't have to. **Less than a third of all small businesses offer any sort of pension plan at all to their employees.** The government has provided very little incentive to invest in employees in the long term.

So if you're an employee of a small business — or any business — what's the lesson here? Save, save, save. You have a lot of tools at your disposal — not just HSAs, but also traditional IRAs, Roth IRAs, and Keogh plans. Use them!

Here's a rundown of current options for setting up a retirement savings plan, whether you're an employee or an employer:
- SEP (Simplified Employee Pension Plan) or SEP-IRA
- Keogh Plan
- 401(k)
- SIMPLE (Savings Incentive Match Plan)
- IRA or Roth IRA

Your business is eligible for SEP, Keogh and SIMPLE plans if you are self-employed, a sole proprietor, a partnership, an S corporation or a C corporation. It is also possible to set up a 401(k) plan for a single person — yourself — as well as for a business group.

A Rising Tide Lifts All Boats

Like HSAs, most retirement plans must be offered to all employees if they're offered to any employees.

If you set up any of these plans through your business, you have to make them available to all employees (another non-discrimination rule). In the past, many small business owners have not made these plans available to their workers. They just set up individual retirement accounts (IRA)s for themselves, and encourage their employees to do the same — on their own time, and on their own dime.

Contributions to all these plans are tax-deductible by the individual taxpayer on the 1040. Interest and earnings are tax-free on the money you put into these retirement accounts, until you reach retirement age. Sound familiar? These qualities are similar to the tax shelter aspects of an HSA.

Definitions

Keogh plans are qualified plans for the self-employed. They cannot be established by an employee; they must be established by the business — even if it's a sole proprietorship. They can include profit-sharing plans, 401(k)s, and certain kinds of pension plans — they correspond very closely with the kinds of employee plans you'd see at large corporations.

Individual Retirement Accounts (IRAs) come in three forms.

A **traditional** IRA is a tax-deferred savings and investment account. You don't pay taxes on its earnings until you withdraw them at retirement age.

A **Roth** IRA reverses the equation: you deposit money on which you've already paid income taxes, but when you withdraw the money — and the account's earnings — it's entirely tax-free. Roth IRAs are somewhat more permissive about when and how you can use your money.

A **SIMPLE** (Savings Incentive Match Plan for Employees) IRA works somewhat like a traditional IRA, but with two important differences: it must be set up by a business, and its contribution limits are higher.

A **SEP** (Simplified Employee Pension) is another option for the self-employed. It must be set up by a business (again, a sole proprietorship qualifies). Its contribution limit is higher than that for a traditional IRA, but lower than that for a 401(k).

The big difference is that if you take out any money from your SEP or Keogh or SIMPLE accounts before you reach age 59 1/2, it's taxable and a 10 percent "early withdrawal" tax penalty applies to the amount you withdrew. With an HSA, there is no penalty for taking out the money when you need it, *as long as it is used for a qualified medical expense.*

Why "Early"?
SEP, Keogh and SIMPLE accounts really are for your retirement — not for now. The early-withdrawal penalty tax is there to encourage you to leave your savings intact until it's time to use them as retirement income.

If you want a tax-advantaged savings vehicle but can foresee some major expenses before retirement — say, a house, or higher education for the kids — consider putting some of your savings in a Roth IRA. You'll pay income taxes on the amounts you deposit — but *not* on the investment growth, and *not* on your withdrawals (distributions). And after five years, regardless of your age, you can withdraw any or all of the money without penalty.

Note that participation in a Roth IRA may limit your ability to contribute to other retirement savings accounts, such as SEPs. You'll need to weigh the advantages of each savings vehicle against your personal situation.

Unlike HSAs, these older, tax-advantaged programs allowed by the federal government are really only suitable for long-range saving. The government would like you to just keep putting money in, and never take it out, until you really decide to retire.

As you develop your HSA strategy, you should monitor your other investments to make sure you have a balanced portfolio. Keep enough money in easily converted form to cover unexpected medical expenses. Your other tax-advantaged accounts should be tapped only in the most extreme emergencies.

As with all investments, **balance** is the keyword. Balance retirement savings with present-day needs. Keep some long-term savings out of reach; keep some emergency money easily accessible (or "liquid") in a more flexible savings vehicle, such as a money-market account.

The Mighty IRA

The traditional Individual Retirement Account, or IRA, recently celebrated its 20th anniversary as the retirement savings plan of choice for millions of Americans. Experimented and tinkered with, honed and polished by legions of tax accountants, it's hard to imagine that IRAs were once as unheard-of as HSAs are today. According to data from the Investment Company Institute in Washington, DC, approximately 60% of all working individuals over the age of 18 have participated in an IRA, and 81% of all working households participate in this or some other form of a defined-contribution retirement benefit plan.

Definitions

A **defined-contribution** plan allows you (or in some cases your employer) to add a certain amount of money every year. The benefit the plan pays depends on how that money grows once it's been invested. Some examples of defined-contribution plans are HSAs, IRAs, and so-called "cash balance" pension plans. You may also have heard of **defined-benefit** plans, which guarantee a certain benefit depending on how you meet certain qualifications. Traditional employer-sponsored pension plans often fall into this category. You're likely to encounter fewer and fewer defined-benefit plans, however. The bursting of the stock market bubble in 2001 revealed weaknesses in this plan structure when plans that had lost major investment worth still had to make good on their promised benefits. The effects of this "shakedown" are still playing out, but be prepared for employers and other plan vendors to lean strongly toward the defined-contribution model.

Any taxpayer with any size income, from a self-employed sole proprietor, to the smallest full-time cog in a vast corporate machine, can open an Individual Retirement Account. As long as you are under 70 1/2 years old, you can open an IRA and make contributions to it this tax year.

IRAs are meant to be long-term savings tools for individual taxpayers. You're not supposed to take the money out until you retire. If you do, serious tax penalties apply.

The "new and improved" form of IRA is called the Roth IRA (named for U.S. Senator William Roth), and some of the better features of the Roth IRA were incorporated in the HSA program.

For those who need a briefing, here are the key elements of a Roth IRA:

- The yearly contribution limit is $3,000 per tax year.
- Your yearly contribution is deducted from your GROSS INCOME.
- Contributions can be as late as April 15 for the previous tax year.
- Catch-up contributions (an extra $500 per year) can be made by individuals 50 or older.
- Earnings accumulate tax-free.
- Distributions made after the taxpayer reaches age 59 1/2, dies, or is disabled qualify as tax-exempt.
- Money must remain "locked up" (that is, unused and in the account) for at least five years before distribution can be qualified as tax-exempt.
- The 10 percent early-withdrawal penalty may be waived for the first $10,000 of withdrawal, if you use that withdrawal for the first-time purchase of a home.
- Rollover rules and requirements are similar to those governing regular IRAs.

HSAs have one big advantage over Roth IRAs as a retirement savings plan. A Roth IRA generally restricts tax-free contributions to a maximum of $3,000. With HSAs, you can shelter more — up to $5,850 in 2005, if you have family coverage under a qualifying high-deductible plan and qualify for catch-up provision. Used in combination with an IRA, Keogh, or 401(k) plan, HSAs are a considerable boost to the total amount of money that can be saved tax-free for retirement — yet can still be used, when necessary, to handle medical emergencies or unforeseen health care costs.

How HSAs May Work with HRAs or FSAs

In the past, companies have offered employer-sponsored flexible spending accounts (FSAs) or Health Reimbursement Accounts (HRAs) to help employees pay for medical costs that might not be covered under their employer-sponsored health insurance plan.

The IRS has issued a series of rulings making it easier to integrate these older programs with HSAs, in part so that employers may be able to phase out these programs and promote HSAs instead.

For example, there are a number of ways that you can participate in an employer-sponsored FSA or HRA and still remain eligible to contribute to a health savings account. IRS Rev. Rule 2004-45 is a ruling clarifying the parameters, and it even suggests a number of scenarios that might arise, showing which benefit combinations would enable you to access benefits from FSAs and HRAs while remaining eligible to contribute to an HSA.

In particular, if you're eligible (and covered by a high-deductible health plan), you may continue to contribute money into an HSA while also being covered by the following types of employer-provided plans that reimburse medical expenses:

(1) Limited-purpose FSAs and HRAs that restrict reimbursements to certain permitted benefits such as vision, dental, or preventive care benefits;

(2) Suspended HRAs, where you have elected to forgo health reimbursements for the coverage period;

(3) Post-deductible FSAs or HRAs that only provide reimbursements after you satisfy the minimum annual deductible; and

(4) Retirement HRAs that only provide reimbursements after an employee retires.

Health Reimbursement Accounts (HRAs) are similar to HSAs, except: Only your employer may contribute to an HRA.

HRAs are generally not portable — that is, you forfeit them if you leave your job. Some employers allow vesting in accumulated HRA balances, but the account is still generally not accessible until you reach retirement age.

Participation in an HRA may be contingent upon participation in specific employer-sponsored health coverage (often, in a so-called "consumer-driven health plan").

For more information on HRAs, look at Chapter One.

Under the ruling, employers may allow employees to temporarily suspend their ability to get reimbursements from HRAs so they can contribute to an HSA, without forfeiting accumulated HRA benefits. The IRS believes that this aspect of the ruling provides important transitional relief for employers and employees wishing to switch to high-deductible health insurance plans that qualify for HSAs.

Certain combinations of these arrangements may be provided without disqualifying a worker from contributing to an HSA. The ruling clarifies that an individual with coverage under an FSA and an HRA, as well as an HSA, may reimburse expenses through the FSA or HRA before taking distributions from the HSA, as long the individual does not seek multiple tax-favored reimbursements for the same expense. In other words, you may not pay for a medical expense with your own HSA dollars, and then expect to be reimbursed through your employer-sponsored HRA.

How HSAs Work with COBRA

Under current law, employees may use HSA funds to pay the premiums for COBRA coverage, as the IRS has deemed this to be a qualifying medical expense.

COBRA is a federal program that currently applies to businesses with more than 20 employees participating in a company-supported health insurance plan. The program covers employees who quit, are fired or laid off, or lose their right to participate in the plan if the business goes bankrupt.

Full-time workers who become part-time workers can also get COBRA if their part-time status makes them ineligible for the company health plan.

COBRA allows these workers to continue receiving health care coverage through the employer for a specified period. Currently this period is 18 months after quitting, firing, or losing hours, and 36 months for more arcane qualifying events. But they can only do so if they pay for the insurance premiums themselves.

By federal law, the premium cost for COBRA coverage must be the same as the group rate. But you'll probably be responsible for paying all of it — not just the 20 or 30 percent you paid as a full-time employee. Employers are also allowed to charge an extra 2 percent, over the group rate, to cover administrative costs at their end. The premium invoices may be mailed out monthly by a COBRA administrator, the usual route for large corporations. Smaller businesses can make arrangements with the departing employee so that he or she will mail back a check each month to cover the premium cost.

What Can Extend Your COBRA Coverage?

Situations such as disability and divorce may allow you to have more than 18 months of COBRA coverage. In these circumstances, different members of your family may be eligible for different lengths of COBRA continuation coverage.

The real question is whether you *want* COBRA coverage for the maximum period available to you. It's almost always more expensive than your employer-sponsored coverage (usually 102% of the premium price, but in some cases of extended coverage as much as 152% — and you pay the whole amount instead of splitting it with your employer). For a healthy individual, COBRA is likely more expensive than individual coverage under a high-deductible health plan.

Hang onto COBRA, though, if you have a condition such as asthma or diabetes — anything that a new insurer might consider pre-existing. Under federal law, if you've had continuous medical coverage, your new insurer can't impose a pre-existing condition limitation on your new coverage. See Chapter Three for more details.

The COBRA Waiver

The continued coverage does not have to be a qualifying high-deductible insurance policy plan; it can be an older form of HMO or PPO.

The reason for this waiver is that COBRA is considered a "temporary" or "transitional" insurance plan, one that phases out when the 18-month period is over, or when the individual decides to drop coverage. As COBRA payments for an HMO may cost hundreds of dollars per month, it seems logical that many who wish to participate in the HSA program will stick with COBRAs only until they can obtain a less expensive qualifying high-deductible insurance policy, either by themselves or through a new employer.

Note for bootstrappers (those who self-finance their ventures): Self-employed persons who have started a business while covered by COBRA through a former employer can still use their HSA account to pay their COBRA premiums. Profile: Shane

A merger left Shane, 49, without the union manufacturing job he'd had for more than half his life. His severance package was decent, but he was blindsided by the cost of COBRA coverage for himself and his wife Carrie.

They have one son, Robert, who's now a junior at the state university. The university offers low-cost indemnity health coverage to its students, so Robert has opted to pay for that with his part-time job rather than ask his parents to continue covering him at COBRA rates. Shane and Carrie do still pay for Robert's room and board, as well as a few incidentals throughout the school year; it costs them about $10,000 per year.

Immediately after being laid off, Shane's first thought was to find another manufacturing job, but now he's not so sure. The industry seems less and less stable; every week he hears of more layoffs across the country. He wants to provide for Carrie, and for their future — they always talked about traveling once Robert moved out of the house — but soon even covering basic expenses may be a problem. The issue isn't working — "I've got years of work left in me," Shane says — it's finding work.

Like so many others who have found themselves unemployed by the New Economy, Shane decides to stop looking for work and start his own business instead. His passion has always been custom motorcycles — he's built three for himself, and Robert uses one of his creations to get around campus — so he decides to try making his passion his full-time occupation. He opens a designer motorcycle service out of his garage.

Shane had been hanging on to his COBRA coverage in the hopes that he could replace it with coverage from a new employer, but now he realizes he'll need to find insurance as an individual. That's not cheap for him — he's a smoker. Carrie has begged him to quit for years, but he's never been able to kick the habit. When he learns that HSAs will allow him to pay for smoking-cessation aids tax-free, he decides he might as well try a few new things at once. He buys a high-deductible health plan for himself and Carrie. The premiums are far lower than his COBRA payments, which means — to his surprise — he might actually be able to save something for retirement in his HSA.

Shane names his new business Reinventing the Wheel. "I'm proof positive that you're never too old to learn new things," he says. After three months he has also managed not to return to smoking. "But you know," he jokes, "now I'm going to have to open another HSA just to pay for the gum I chew."

How HSAs Work with Unemployment Benefits

Employers have no obligation under current federal unemployment laws that relate to contributions or distributions from HSAs. If you've quit or been fired, your employer-sponsored HSA is still yours, but your employer won't contribute to it any more. You may want to roll that account over to one with a bank of your choosing, so you have more control over its administration.

Unemployed workers who do not qualify for COBRA may opt to purchase a temporary health insurance policy. Many states make this option available. Under current law, you may use HSA funds to pay the premiums for this kind of temporary policy, but only as long as you continue to receive unemployment payment benefits (anywhere from six to 18 months).

Retirement Issues and Social Security

Under recently released regulations, if you're over 65 but haven't actually applied to receive Medicare Part A or B, you may still contribute to an HSA. You also continue to qualify for catch-up contributions. Once you being receiving Medicare or Social Security benefits, you're no longer allowed to contribute to your HSA. However, no law says you have to spend that money right away. You're free to let your investment continue growing.

Employees who "officially retire"earlier than age 65 may continue contributing on their own to existing HSAs until they begin receiving Social Security or Medicare, if they choose to start a small business of their own in the interim.

Employees younger than age 65 who become eligible for Social Security benefits for any reason are likewise restricted from opening new HSAs or from contributing money to their existing HSAs.

Using HSAs to Fund Long-Term Care Insurance

The legislation provides that funds from an HSA can be used to reimburse premiums paid for a qualified long-term care (LTC) insurance plan. LTC premium payments can be treated as tax-free distributions, like other qualified medical expenses. By using HSA funds in this way, employees can in effect, look ahead to their needs in their retirement years, and pay for their long term care insurance using pre-tax dollars.

For purchasers of long-term-care insurance, this is a tax advantage over the way LTC premiums are paid for today. Most employees covered by a workplace health insurance policy are not eligible for that deduction on their personal income tax simply because their total medical expenses don't meet the floor for medical expenses, 7.5% of adjusted gross income.

INTEGRATING HSAs: THE BASICS

HSAs can serve as a second tax-free retirement account.

HSAs resemble and expand the benefits of Roth IRAs.

IRS rulings are making it easier to integrate FSAs, HRAs, dental plans and retirement benefits with an HSA strategy.

Employers are not obligated to continue benefits to workers who quit or get fired or laid off.

HSAs can be used to fund COBRA insurance costs.

If you retire before age 65, you may still contribute to an HSA under certain circumstances.

Your Timetable and Plan

2

This chapter is a checklist of what to do when; it will take you step by step into either (A) starting a new health plan with HSAs or (B) converting an old one to take advantage of HSAs.

For the uninsured and the underinsured — or anyone concerned about the rising costs of health care — the federal program for HSAs is a welcome option. Starting the program for yourself or for your own small business can be managed is as few as ten easy steps.

CHECKLIST FOR INDIVIDUALS: ENROLLING IN A NEW HEALTH BENE-FIT PLAN

Analyze Your Needs and Find a Vendor

_____1. Gather relevant eligibility data and financial materials from the previous tax year. [Estimated work time: 1/2 hour or less] (This includes copies of your personal 1040 or 1040A tax forms and any other relevant filings.)

_____2. Gather relevant data from your health expenses from the previous tax year. [Estimated work time: 1/2 hour or less] (This includes records of premium payments; checkbook notations for doctor co-pays or doctor visits; receipts for out-of-pocket and unreimbursed expenses for medical care, equipment, prescription drugs, treatments, and over-the-counter medications.)

_____3. Set aside some time to complete Worksheet #1 in Chapter 2 to determine your complete health care costs (premiums and

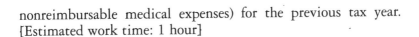

nonreimbursable medical expenses) for the previous tax year. [Estimated work time: 1 hour]

_____4. Research insurance vendors. [Estimated work time: 4 hours]

(Make it your goal to examine the offerings of at least five different vendors within your state that offer HSA-qualifying high-deductible policies. You may wish to review Chapter 3 for tips on investigating vendors. To get you started, the website created for this book, www.HSAfinder.com, leads you to updated lists of providers of HSA-qualifying insurance policies in all 50 states.)

_____5. Request policies from the five vendors so you may compare them. After comparing, choose at least three for further investigation. If you are working with a broker, have the broker assemble the materials for your review. [Estimated work time: 1 hour]

_____6. Do the numbers. Go back to Chapter 2, and finish filling out the applicable worksheet to determine the most cost-effective vendor and policy plans for your situation. [Estimated work time: 1–2 hours]

_____7. If you use a tax accountant, discuss the tax ramifications of deductions for insurance premium costs, administrative costs, and contributions to HSAs. [Estimated work time: 1–2 hours]

(Seeking advice from a competent business tax professional is highly recommended at this stage. You may also wish to review Chapter 7 for tips on where to find deductions for personal taxes.)

_____8. Research HSA custodians (banks and other vendors) to manage contributions and withdrawals for your personal account. [Estimated work time: 4–8 hours]

(Review Chapter 4 for tips on selecting custodian vendors. Consider vendors already partnering with your top three insurance picks if there is potential for administrative economies or ease of use. To get you started, the website created for this book, www.HSAfinder.com, leads you to a list of HSA account vendors, including those with a track record of handling MSAs during the pilot phase.)

_____9. Make your selection of both an insurance policy vendor and HSA account bank or account custodian. [Estimated work time: 1–2 hours]

(Review all contracts and agreements before signing. If you have any questions about service levels or guarantees, now is the time to ask!)

_____10. Congratulations! You are now ready to enjoy the tax-advantaged benefits of a low-cost and effective health insurance program!

CHECKLIST FOR THE SELF-EMPLOYED AND THE SMALL-BUSINESS OWNER: LAUNCHING A NEW HEALTH BENEFIT PLAN FOR YOUR BUSINESS

Phase One: Needs Analysis and Vendor Search

_____1. Gather relevant eligibility data and financial materials from the previous tax year. [Estimated work time: 1/2 hour or less]

(This includes: copies of your personal 1040 or 1040A tax form; Schedule C, Schedule SE, and other relevant filings for your sole proprietorship, partnership, LLC, LLP, C or S Corporation.)

_____2. Gather relevant data from your health expenses (as a business and/or as an individual) from the previous tax year. [Estimated work time: 1/2 hour or less]

(This includes: records of premium payments; checkbook notations for doctor co-pays or doctor visits; receipts for out-of-pocket and unreimbursed expenses for medical care, equipment, prescription drugs, treatments, and over-the-counter medications.)

_____3. Set aside some time to complete at least the first part of Worksheet #1 (if you are self-employed and have no employees) or Worksheet #2 (if you have employees) in Chapter 2 to determine your complete health care costs (premiums and nonreimbursable medical expenses) for the previous tax year. [Estimated work time: 1 hour]

_____4. Research insurance vendors. [Estimated work time: 4 hours]

(Make it your goal to examine the offerings of at least five different vendors within your state that offer HSA-qualifying high-deductible policies. You may wish to review Chapter 3 for tips on investigating vendors. To get you started, the website created for this book, www.HSAfinder.com, leads you to updated lists of providers of HSA qualifying insurance policies in all 50 states.)

_____5. Request policies from the five vendors so you may compare them. After comparing, choose at least three for further investigation. If you are working with a broker, have the broker assemble the materials for your review. [Estimated work time: 1 hour]

(Remember that if you do not have a health insurance benefit plan in place for your employees, it is perfectly acceptable to offer *only* two high-deductible plans: one for singles, and one for family coverage, provided that your state does not also require you to offer an HMO as well. You may also choose a single deductible figure in the middle range for both groups ($2,000-$5,000) for simplicity's sake; this may not be practical — or fair — if you employ both low-wage workers and high-salaried staff.)

_____6. Do the numbers. Go back to Chapter 2, and finish filling out the applicable worksheet to determine the most cost-effective vendor and policy plans for your situation. [Estimated work time: 1–2 hours]

(If you anticipate contributing money to employee HSA accounts, review Chapter 5 for details on contribution limits and other restrictions and regulations such as the non-discrimination rule and rules for workers over 55.)

_____7. If you use a tax accountant, payroll administrator, or business tax advisor, discuss the tax ramifications of business deductions for insurance premium costs, administrative costs, and contributions to worker HSAs from business monies. [Estimated work time: 1–2 hours]

(Seeking advice from a competent business tax professional is highly recommended at this stage. You may also wish to review Chapter 7 for tips on where to find deductions for personal and business taxes.)

_____8. Research HSA custodians (banks and other vendors) to manage contributions and withdrawals to be recommended as the initial custodian for employee accounts. [Estimated work time: 4–8 hours]

4 for tips on selecting custodian vendors. Vendors
g with your top three insurance picks should be con-
potential for administrative economies or ease of use.
started, the website created for this book,
w .....   .com, leads you to a list of HSA account vendors,
including those with a track record of handling MSAs during the pilot
phase.)

_____9. Make your selection of both an insurance policy vendor and
HSA account bank or account custodian. [Estimated work time:
1–2 hours]

(Review all contracts and agreements before signing. If you have any
questions about service levels or guarantees, now is the time to ask!)

_____10. Congratulations! If you are self-employed, or a sole propri-
etor with no employees besides a spouse or other family member,
you are now ready to enjoy the tax-advantaged benefits of a low-
cost and effective health insurance program! If you have employees, proceed to the checklist in Appendix C for phase two of your
approach.

THE HRA "THREE-STEP"

One of the stumbling blocks for businesses that employ low-wage
workers is the very real fact that low-wage earners may find it difficult
to pay out several thousand dollars in medical expenses until their
deductible level has been met.

One solution that's been proposed for those who will self-insure their
employees is to set up a Health Reimbursement Plan (HRA) to supplement what the business or the worker can contribute to an HSA.

As of publication, it's not entirely clear how the IRS will allow HRAs
to be "stacked" between an employer-funded HSA and the deductible
limit of the high-deductible insurance policy. What does appear to be
permissible is employer reimbursement for co-insurance after the
deductible is met. In other words, a worker with an individual policy
carrying a $2,500 deductible and a $5,100 out-of-pocket maximum in
2005 (for any coinsurance beyond the deductible) might be given
$500 in a employer HSA contribution; the worker would be responsi-

ble for the next $2,000 in expenses up to the deductible limit, and might then be able to apply to the employer for health reimbursement (through an HRA plan) for any sums paid out for coinsurance after the year's deductible had been met.

Under this scenario, some very basic health expenses can be paid for, and major medical problems are provided for. Within the middle ground, however, the worker may be expected to be thrifty about additional expenses if they come out of his or her own wallet. Adding an HRA to the benefits mix can help workers become better health care consumers — in theory at least. While health reimbursements under an HRA plan do not have to be funded until the employee asks for reimbursement, good plan designs should assume that all participating workers will "max out" or deplete all the money that's been set aside for this benefit.

ORGANIZING YOUR PLAN: THE BASICS

- The key to successful implementation of your new HSA plan in communication and organization.

- Make a plan and commit it to paper.

- Create a timetable and stick to it.

- Assign tasks and follow-up frequently.

- Communicate regularly with all involved parties; check progress.

- Celebrate completion.

Conclusion

Conclusions and Future Trends: Are HSAs the Next IRAs?

With the experience gained so far in purchasing and using HSAs, it is evident that many individuals are embracing them. The debate over health care funding is continuing and there is great division as to the best way of fixing the system. No one can doubt that health care costs are increasing at double-digit rates, or that the health insurance premiums for employees are generally outpacing these rate raises as well. What is in doubt, is the best way of slowing it down. HSAs clearly are working as an avenue.

In the past, employers paid the true costs of medical services for their employees, in the form of ever-rising health insurance premiums. Today, the burden of rising premium costs is being shifted to employees. And now that employees are being required to pay a larger share of their premiums, many have come to see the price they pay for health care insurance through the workplace is too high. HSAs are an answer that is coming at the right time.

For my first book, Houston economist, Dr. Kenneth E. Lehrer, projected these trends:
- Jobs will become much less permanent
- Outsourcing, aside from international outsourcing, will grow
- Independent contracting will proliferate
- Telecommuting will become an accepted career alternative at all income levels.

As this book goes to press, he continues to postulate this evolving society will clearly create a demand on the part of workers for not just more affordable health care, but more portable health insurance, up to and including the associated and aligned medical or retirement benefits you will personally carry with them from job to job.

While an HSA cannot solve all of these career-centered issues, its flexibility and adaptability should make a positive contribution in fulfilling existing gaps facing workers and their health care demands.

Through HSAs, employees will be able to create their own, in Lehrer's words, "medical financial storehouse." As a result, the negative effects of career changes, multiple jobs, and independent contracting could decline as a significant hurdle to fulfilling an individual's health care needs.

Seeking to project an HSA adoption rate, Lehrer postulates that over time, like IRAs and 401(k)s, HSAs should reach a level of more than 20 million individuals by the fourth quarter of 2006. The nation's experience today is ratifying Dr. Lehrer's hypothesis.

health care Premiums Exceed Costs

HSAs arrive, Lehrer argues, at an opportune time. It is clear that tax-delayed retirement programs, such as Keoghs and Roth IRAs, have become a part of the country's compensation system. According to data from the Investment Company Institute is Washington, D.C., approximately 60% of all working individuals over the age of 18 participate in an IRA, 60% in a 401(k) plan, and 81% of all working households participate in some form of a defined contribution retirement benefit plan.

Therefore, Lehrer argues, HSAs can be an attractive alternative for individuals as well as employees besides being a vehicle for reducing employer health care costs.

Healthy workers will opt for high-deductible insurance programs. These often are the most cost-effective for insurance companies as well as for individuals.

Insurance companies and corporate officials acknowledge that the 20-80 rule seems to work in health care programs as in many other situations. That is, 20 percent of a company's workers are responsible for 80 percent of medical claims. Critics fear that the healthiest workers will opt out of regular health care programs, leaving those programs burdened with the sickest (and therefore most expensive) participants. To slow the rise in health care costs and rein in rate increases, critics and proponents alike are suggesting the development of a "consumer" model that puts more of the health care choices in the hands of workers.

The banner for all these initiatives has a common name: "consumer-direct health care." This, then, is a "user" model that can work. With HSAs, true health care costs become very apparent to the individual who writes the check and will later be reimbursed with his or her own dollars.

Dr. Lehrer suggests that the current economic environment is remarkably different from that of 1996, when HSAs were originally launched under a pilot program and called Medical Savings Accounts (MSAs or Archer Savings Accounts).

The program was authorized only to 1.5 million American small businesses and self-employed individuals. By 2000, the initial program proved to be a cost saver and a responsible method for individuals and families to control their own health care expenses.

Today, as Dr. Lehrer points out in his analysis, there are several other aspects associated with HSAs that will encourage early adoption at a rate unseen in previous situations.

Just as credit cards has become closely tied to checking accounts and, in many cases, can automatically be drawn against brokerage account margin balances, it is only a matter of time, creativity and potentially some additional legislation that will allow an HSA to be another weapon in the arsenal of household financial planning.

In the end, it is up to the individual to choose his or her method of providing for health care. Many believe the majority of eligible individuals will opt for HSAs once the public gets to know the costs of alternatives and the benefits of these new offerings.

How big is this marketplace? Statistics indicate that the present workforce, excluding farms, comprises approximately 148 million individuals. These employees are grouped into approximately 25 million firms, including sole proprietorships, partnerships and corporations of all sizes. Lehrer, relying upon the initial commencement rate of 10% of all firms utilizing HSAs is realistic. This will then equate to approximately 2.5 million organizations with a projected payroll of 20 million individuals initially being covered under HSA plans by the fourth quarter 2006.

Assuming an average retention rate of $600 for each account, this potentially puts more than $12 billion under HSA account management by the end of 2006.

There are pitfalls as well as opportunities here. Some critics argue that the untaxed portion (at an effective rate of 20 percent) would mean $12 billion in lost tax receipts. For insurers (including Medicare) there's the promise that consumer-directed programs will save that much, or more, by eliminating or reducing double-billing and insurance fraud.

Are HSAs the panacea for everything that is wrong with health insurance? Of course not.

Can they help employers and employees alike break this spiraling cycle of rising costs? Probably yes.

Will they have a financial and social impact on America? Very definitely. The road is before us. Many of us will need to take it.

Appendices: More Guidelines For Small Businesses

APPENDIX A:
Setting Up Your Payroll for HSAs

Employer Contributions

Employer deposits to HSAs can be set up like any other payroll savings plan. Custodian banks with experience managing medical savings accounts (MSAs) may be the most adept at handling electronic transfers of funds from your business into individual HSA accounts. Naturally, this works better if all workers have their HSAs with the same custodian or bank. But even if workers choose other custodians, these custodial vendors should be able to provide the employee with the necessary forms to enroll and obtain permission for payroll deductions.

Pay stubs should detail HSA contributions for each pay period. If you also indicate total HSA deposits for the year, this information will be extremely helpful for anyone trying to keep within the contribution limit. For employees who prefer direct deposit, printable electronic statements, or a printed stub reflecting contributions can be a very useful tool.

On pay stubs and with W-2 reporting, *employer* contributions to work-

---

Hiring Family Members

Under current law, you must pay FICA but do not have to pay unemployment insurance (FUTA) on the salary of a spouse or parent that works in your business. If your child works for you and is under 18 years of age, you don't have to pay FICA or FUTA.

er HSAs will be entered as "non-wage" compensation (in Box 12 on the W-2). As we've discussed, these amounts are not subject to withholding of income tax, FICA or FUTA. The employer gets the tax deduction as well.

An *employee's* contribution into an HSA, even if it is the form of elective amounts deposited from wages through an automatic savings plan, must be included in income as wages on the W-2 and so will be subject to income tax withholding, Social Security and Medicare taxes. The employer gets no tax relief and no benefits; the employee may take the deduction on his or her personal income tax.
It might be prudent for an employer to offer employees a contribution to their HSAs in lieu of a raise. This is permissible, but only if all workers with an HSA are also given the same proportional non-wage adjustment. The advantage to the employer is avoidance of payroll taxes on the additional salary. As always, when in doubt, consult your tax accountant or financial advisor.

For more information on HSAs and business tax deductions, see Chapter 7, "Realizing the Tax Advantages of an HSA."

Basic First Steps (Checklist)

___ Obtain Employer Identification Number (EIN) for your business. You must do this if you plan to pay wages to at least one other person beside yourself. To apply for a number, use IRS form SS-4. You can do this online.

___ Decide how frequently you'll issue paychecks (Weekly? Biweekly? Monthly?).

___ Decide which of your workers are full time employees. Some of your help may wish to be paid as independent contractors, if eligible.

___ Obtain a completed withholding application (W-4 form), Social Security Number, for each employee.

___ Make a note to file 1099s for each independent contractor you expect to pay more than $600 in this tax year.

Who Is an Employee?

You can only deduct, as a legitimate business expense, your cost of health insurance premiums for workers who are employees. This can include part-time as well as full-time workers. The IRS tracks these contributions, along with wages you've paid and income taxes withheld, on the W-2 form filed for each worker.

Payments to independent contractors and freelancers and some part-time help are tracked to the IRS with a 1099 form, rather than W-2. The 1099 is an "exemption from withholding" — a notice to the IRS that you are not paying Social Security and Medicare on that person's behalf. The independent contractor is responsible for these personal taxes and any income tax.

It is possible for an entrepreneur to jointly set up a "group" to obtain health insurance for valued freelancers or independent contractors, with some IRS tax relief if you, the company owner, pay for any of their health insurance costs. However, self-employed freelancers may be able to deduct 100 percent of the costs of the premiums from their self-employment earnings, but only if they pay the entire cost for their own premiums. Thus, the independent contractors may always be encouraged to pay for their own insurance premiums, even if your company provides the plan.

If you're not sure whether a worker should be getting a 1099 or a W-2, look up IRS Publication #15 (Employer's Tax Guide), which gives these rules in detail. The IRS generally defines an employee as someone who works exclusively for you, and who works at your place of business (or telecommutes) and keeps regular hours.

If you are starting or formalizing a business, decide which members of your team qualify as employees, and play by the withholding rules. The IRS penalties for pretending an employee is just a contract worker are very steep.

Excluding Contributions From an Employee's Taxable Income

On a payroll you must calculate withholding in accordance with government tables to cover the employee's income tax. Federal Income Tax requires this withholding, as do the majority of states that have State and/or Local Income Tax. Contributions to HSAs on behalf of employees are exempt from these taxes, and join the list of other forms of worker compensation that are not taxed:

- Generally all health coverage policy premiums
- Generally all employer contributions to employee retirement plans
- All worker's compensation premiums or benefits
- Extra sick pay or disability (after the first six months)
- Reimbursements for moving expenses, parking garages, public transit (subject to certain limits)
- Reimbursements for business expenses by employees (T & E) when these are accounted for to the employer

More Tax Relief for Employers

In addition to withholding for income tax, you must withhold a percentage of each employee's pay for Social Security and Medicare under The Federal Insurance Contributions Act (otherwise known as FICA) towards the benefits they will one day receive from Social Security and Medicare.

In tax year 2005, the tax rate of a paycheck is 7.65%:
- 6.20 percent for Social Security
- 1.45 percent for Medicare

But wait, there's more: as an employer, you must also pay an equal amount of taxes to the government on behalf of the employee. You pay the employer's share of FICA on behalf of each worker.

For highly paid employees, there is a FICA ceiling. For tax year 2005, you do not have to pay FICA once you've paid the first $90,000 in wages. There is no Medicare ceiling; no matter what you pay your highest-paid worker, you still have to take out the Medicare tax.

Under the HSA program, **employer contributions to worker HSAs are not subject to any of these taxes**, nor are they considered to be gross wages when calculating a variety of other taxes, such as Withholding Unemployment Tax (FUTA). Unemployment tax benefits are regulated by a combined state and federal program. Just like income tax, you have to withhold both a federal tax (FUTA) and a state unemployment tax. The current percentage for federal withholding for FUTA is 6.2%. It is a single flat rate, paid up to a ceiling on the first $7,000 of a worker's pay.

Your state unemployment tax rate will vary from state to state. You may also have to pay Disability Insurance Tax. In certain states (notably New York and California) this is a tax that pays for a mandated state disability insurance program; the employer must withhold such a tax. Under current federal rules, employer contributions to worker HSAs are exempted from these taxes as well.

Working with the W-2

Each employee gets a W-2 by January 31 for the previous tax year. Copies of each employee's form are also sent to the IRS in early February, along with a summary sheet, the Transmittal of Wage and Tax Statements, also known as IRS Form W-3. Employees who leave your company before the tax year is over may also request a copy of their W-2 earlier, so they can see what the total taxes were relating to their employment.

The illustration shows what the W-2 form looks like for the 2004 Tax Year on page 143. It is larger and arranged slightly differently from previous forms. Sections a–f identify the employee by name, address, and Social Security number. (The "control number" is an option for employers who keep track of many workers by employee number.)

Wages (plus tips and compensation) for each employee are totaled for the year in Box 1. The amount of wages subject to Social Security (the first $87,900 of wages) goes into Box 3. The amount of wages subject to Medicare tax (everything after the first $400) goes into Box 5.

The amount of withholding for each tax (Box 2, 4, 6) should equal the amount you've already paid in monthly and quarterly installments. For how to calculate withholding, see IRS publication #15-T.

Not everyone will use Boxes 7-11. These report Social Security paid on tips and gratuities, and hardship advances for those who will qualify for the Earned Income Tax Credit (EIC).

"Dependent Care Benefits" related to flexible spending accounts; note the amount the company has invested into an employee's FSA or cafeteria plan. (For more on FSAs, see IRS Publication #15-B or Chapter One of this book.)

"Non-Qualified Plans" are other payouts made by the employer on behalf of the employee that may not be tax-exempt from FICA or other payroll taxes. These include distributions from pension plans, IRAs, and profit-sharing plans. For example, if an employee leaves and "cashes out" vested pension funds, the sum is noted on the W-2, and the employee will be responsible for the taxes.

Where then, are the deductions for a company's contributions to an employee's HSA? They are tucked away in Box 12, and identified with a special code "W."

Under Code "W"
Box 12 is the section reserved for payments that generally will be exempt from gross income, and hence from gross income taxes. These include income deferred via a 401(k) plan (Code "D"), Moving Expenses (Code "P") and salary reductions to a SIMPLE (Code "S").

Employer contributions to a Health Savings Account are Code "W." So, in Box 12, if you made a $200 contribution to a worker's HSA, you'll indicate this by "200.00 W."

If you do a W-2 for yourself or a spouse, this is where you will indicate your contribution to your own HSAs. If you contributed $4,500 to your HSA, write down "4500.00 W".

On the employee's tax return, any figure that appears in Box 12 must be matched up as a pre-tax adjustment on the 1040. This is how the IRS will track HSA deductions. This is how they make sure that when the employer makes the contribution, only the employer gets the tax benefits.

Box 13 requires you to check off squares if the worker was exempt from any withholding (as in the case of a part-time worker or an agent paid only by commissions), or "actively participated" in any qualified pension, profit-sharing, or stock-bonus plan, including 401(k), SEP or SIMPLE plans. (Again, this is an IRS match point.)

Box 14 is reserved for other adjustments, which are non-elective, such as required employer-employee matching contributions to pension plans. Another match point. Boxes 15–20 are where you report wages and withholding payments for state and local tax.

This should get you and your payroll administrator up to speed on HSAs.

APPENDIX B:
More On Employee Benefits

The Non-Discrimination Rule
Calculating Contributions On Behalf of Employees

To save money, and a few headaches, you may choose to let all your employees do their own contributions to their own HSA accounts. You can still deduct the amount you contribute for yourself out of your own salary — and deduct that amount from your own taxable income. They, also, can deduct the amount of their contribution from their taxable income on their individual tax returns.

Remember, you don't have to contribute into any employee's HSA account if you don't take a business deduction for the amounts you contribute to your own HSA funding. But if you do pay into your HSA account with money from your business, and pay at least a part of everyone's health care premiums through the company insurance plan, you will have to pay a "comparable" amount into the HSA accounts of all employees who have HSAs, and whose benefit plan is "comparable" to your own.

The simplest solution the law provides is to give each employee, and each boss, an identical contribution. Everyone, for example, gets $200 contributed by the business to his or her HSAs. A simplified way to do this in payroll accounting would be to include the contribution as a "bonus" in compensation at the end of the calendar year.

But this works best if everyone has the same deductible amount on his or her policy. In other words, if all employees signed up for a $2,000 deductible health insurance policy (either as individuals or under a family plan) a $200 contribution for all employees would meet the IRS guidelines.

However, this won't work if employees have chosen different deductible limits. If Alan from accounting chose a $3,000 family deductible policy, and Mary from marketing chose a $2,000 individual deductible policy, a $200 contribution to both Alan and Mary would not be considered a "comparable" contribution by the IRS.

This is where the largess of employer contributions gets tricky. How can a business fairly contribute different amounts to different employees, and still meet the comparability rule?

Since contributions are to a large extent determined by the deductible limit of each person's health insurance policy, the amounts contributed to employees holding $1,000, $1,500, or $3,000 policies should logically be different. In this case, what the law wants is that each contribution be an equal "percentage" of each deductible. In other words, a comparable arrangement would mandate something like this:

For employee with $1,000 individual deductible: $200 contribution
For employee with $1,500 individual deductible: $300 contribution
For employee with $3,000 family deductible: $600 contribution

Here, the contribution for all employees is 20 percent of their deductible. It is a comparable percentage that is fair to all.

For employers already offering benefits through cafeteria plans, or rollovers from existing MSA plans or other HSAs, the comparability rule does not apply.

To better manage HSA contributions for new benefit plans, employers may wish to limit the choices of deductible ranges. If you have not previously offered a health insurance benefit, consider only offering two policy plans: a $2,500 individual policy, and a $2,500 family policy. Under this strategy, the employer's contribution from year to year could safely be an identical dollar amount for all participants in the plan. Between the minimum deductible for families ($2,000) and the maximum for singles ($5,000) there is a good bit of leeway, so you may be able to come up with a figure that satisfies both employee groups. This can allow the true cost of contributing to employee HSAs to be predicted much more easily. (See Chapter 3, "Picking The Right High-Deductible Insurance Plan.")

WARNING: BEWARE THE NON-DISCRIMINATION TAX PENALTY

A stiff IRS tax penalty hits employers who fail to provide "comparable" contributions. The current fine for violations is an excise tax of 35 percent of the TOTAL of all amounts contributed by the employer. Thus, if John and Jill (from the Hat Store example in Chapter Five) both have individual HIGH DEDUCTIBLE policies with the same deductible ($2,000), and John contributes $500 to his own HSA through his business, but fails to contribute a comparable amount to Jill's, the fine will be 35 percent of $500, or $175.

If John had a larger enterprise, and devoted $50,000 to contributions to employee HSA accounts, but failed to divide up the money "comparably" among all participating employees, the IRS could hit John's business with a fine of $17,500.

Make Employees Pay at Least Part of Their Own Premiums

If you're starting a new benefits program, or just adjusting an old one to take advantage of the HSAs, remember it is not written in stone that you, the employer, have to pay the entire cost for monthly premiums. If you feel you can't afford this level of benefits for your workers, you can still offer a health insurance plan but require that employees pay some — or even all — of the premium costs by themselves.

If you are only offering a high-deductible insurance policy plan, the premium costs can be quite low, and affordable to even your lowest-paid workers. Many companies split the cost of premiums, 50-50, with employees. You can make your own split to suit you. For everyone's convenience you can also arrange for his or her share of the premium to be paid as a payroll deduction.

Other Options for the Boss

As long as the non-discrimination rule is honored, employer contributions have considerable flexibility:
- Employer contributions can be treated as a year-end bonus.
- Employer contributions can be contingent on company-wide profit
      or performance goals (but not distributed as profit-sharing).

- Employer contributions can be discontinued in a bad year.
- Employer contributions can be made in January, February, March — even as late as April 15 for the previous tax year.

This last strategy allows the employer to contribute a final, total amount that will produce a significant business-tax write-off that directly addresses the needs of the past tax year (see Chapter Seven).

Cutting Off Contributions and Benefits When Employees Leave

As an employer, you do not have to continue to contribute to employee HSAs once the worker leaves your employ for any reason. As a portable benefit, HSAs are portable to the individual. Workers who are laid off, fired, or quit jobs have been given certain incentives by the Federal government, to encourage them to continue funding their health care needs through this program.

Documentation

As an employer, keep documentation on file that shows when a worker left your employ. If you do not have a departure (i.e., termination) package to give the employee, a simple letter of notice, mailed to the employee's home address, with a copy kept for your files, should suffice as backup in the event the IRS asks for it.

If employee deductions, employer contributions, or employee payments for health policy premiums were made through a payroll savings mechanism, a copy of the documentation sent to the bank of record should also be kept on file.

At the end of the tax year, you will be required to file a W-2 for the former employee, and can note your contributions as "non-wage" compensation.

If you have employees, you're ready to move on to the next phase: communicating the advantages of the HSA program to your workers so they may also benefit from health insurance coverage.

APPENDIX C:
Communicating the Program to Employees

_____1. Check with your insurance vendor about any minimum participation level required for service. Ask the vendor to supply you with several sets of sample materials that may be used to create an information packet for your employees. {Estimated work time: 1/4 hour}

(Participation levels give you a goal to shoot for: you may need 20, 30, or 50 employees signed up before you can effectively launch this health insurance benefit. If workers primarily use a language other than English, ask your vendor for language-appropriate materials.)

_____2. Brainstorm with relevant staff, including human resources, payroll chiefs, office manager, business manager, and worker team leaders as to the best way to promote HSAs to your particular employee pool. {Estimated work time: 2–4 hours}

(You may wish to bring some general demographic data results from your Worksheet #2 (page 183) calculations to the brainstorming meeting if you have more than 20 employees. It is not advisable to show or bring the actual worksheets as they may include personal or confidential information about individual workers.)

_____3. Assign or appoint someone to draft a written explanation of your benefits plan, including a brief introductory brochure that explains the health insurance policies available and retirement savings advantages of HSAs, drawing on both the vendor sample materials and insights from the brainstorming session. {Estimated work time: 1/2 hour}

(If you're not drafting the document yourself, don't allow the assigned staffer to drag their feet on creation of a draft document. Set a firm deadline for the draft, and make sure they have contact numbers for your vendor liaisons and relevant sample materials.)

_____4. Refine the short brochure and the benefits explanation sheets. Show early versions to your brainstorming team for feedback. [Estimated time: up to one week]

(Marketing staff designers and copywriters already working with you should be brought in at this stage, to make sure the materials suit the internal image (i.e., brand identity) of your company. At this point, many businesses will turn over the creation of polished materials to an outside marketing communications professional familiar with their company culture.)

_____5. Distribute the brochure to employees and set up meetings to discuss the new benefits plan. [Estimated time: one to two weeks]

_____6. Prepare a presentation in a format appropriate to your worker pool. Department meetings, small work team meetings, or large group meetings are some of your options. Presentations should last no more than 10 minutes, to allow plenty of time for questions. [Estimated work time: 2–4 hours]

(Meetings should include distribution of the benefits explanation sheets and, always, a referral to a designated staffer if any employee requests information. Make use of e-mail, Internet access, company website FAQs and vendor customer service — accessible websites or toll-free numbers — to enhance your message.

_____7. Set up a deadline for health insurance benefits enrollment.

(Choose the middle of the month for your deadline, as the first of the month and the end of a month can be stressful periods at work. The extra two weeks should also allow you to bring any fence-sitters into the program, and still start your benefits period at a time most convenient to your business needs.)

_____8. There is no need to set up an HSA account benefits deadline if employees will be setting up their own custodial accounts. If you plan to offer employer contributions, a payroll savings plan, direct deposit, or if you will be helping them set up HSAs through a partnered vendor, it may be useful to set a deadline for this participation.

(Some deadline suggestions: four weeks after the health insurance enrollment deadline; December 31 of your current tax year.)

_____9. Monitor the enrollment period to make sure ALL employees are offered the opportunity to participate in both the health insurance policy plan, and HSAs, if they meet eligibility requirements. [Estimated time: 4–6 weeks]

(Non-discrimination policies in many states mandate that all employees be offered a health care benefit; as far as HSAs are concerned, all employees should be informed of their eligibility to participate, particularly if employers will be contributing funds, in order to fully satisfy the non-discrimination rules for HSAs.)

_____10. Refine the program, the brochures, the message, the response to questions, incentives as required, to gain the participation levels that suit your business needs. [Estimated time: 6 months to a year]

(Additional, updates and tips for maximizing business tax advantages through the HSA program are available on the website created for this book.)

☐ ☐ ☐ ☐ ☐ ☐

Calculating The Cost Savings Of A High-Deductible health care Plan

Total Spent in Health Insurance Premiums for all employees, Previous Year

Divide by total number of employees covered by plan

Equals TOTAL Y (Insurance Cost Per Employee)

Estimated Total X for High-Deductible Insurance Premiums in New Year, for one employee

Subtract "X" from "Y" to get estimated cost savings for each employee converting to HD plan, New Year:

Multiply "C" by number of employees (see page 51) to estimate potential savings if all employees convert to HD

WORKSHEET #2

APPENDIX D:
Converting an Existing Benefits Plan for the HSA Program

Companies wishing to wean employees off costly full-benefit insurance plans may have to take it slowly or will face resistance. Smart business leaders will anticipate both internal and external hurdles well in advance of preparing an internal marketing program that can be used to "sell" employees on HSAs.

Phase One: Needs Analysis and Vendor Search

_____1. Gather relevant eligibility data and financial materials from the previous tax year. Payroll tax summaries and breakdowns should be included, along with union regulations that may affect eligibility or program choice. [Estimated work time: 2 hours or less]

(This includes: copies of relevant personal and business tax forms; (Schedule C, Schedule SE, and other relevant filings for your sole proprietorship, partnership, LLC, LLP, C or S Corporation.)

_____2. Gather relevant data on your health expenses (as a business) from the previous tax year. Year-end summaries from all your benefits vendors (including retirement programs as well as health programs) are a must. [Estimated work time: 2 hours or less]

(This includes: administrative costs from your current benefit vendors; records of premium payments; participation levels, customer service satisfaction records, etc.)

_____3. Set aside some time to complete at least the first part of Worksheet #2 in Chapter 2 to determine your complete health care costs as an employer for the previous tax year. [Estimated work time: 1 hour]

_____4. Research insurance vendors. [Estimated work time: 4 hours]

(Notify your current health insurance that you plan to offer HSA-qualifying high-deductible policies to your employees this year. You may wish to review Chapter 3 for tips on identifying additional vendors. To get you started, the website created for this book, www.HSAfinder.com, leads you to updated lists of providers of HSA-qualifying insurance policies in all 50 states.)

_____5. Request policies from at least three vendors so you may compare them. If you are working with a broker, have the broker assemble the materials for your review. [Estimated work time: 1 hour]

(Do not allow your existing vendor or broker to procrastinate about creating a qualifying policy plan — set a reasonable but firm deadline, and be prepared to switch vendors if necessary.)

_____6. Do the numbers. Go back to Chapter 2, and finish filling out the applicable worksheet to determine the most cost-effective vendor and policy plans for your situation. [Estimated work time: 2–4 hours]

(If you anticipate contributing money to employee HSA accounts, review Chapter 5 for details on contribution limits and other restrictions and regulations such as the non-discrimination rule and rules for workers over 55.)

_____7. If you use a tax accountant, payroll administrator, or business tax advisor, discuss the tax ramifications of business deductions for insurance premium costs, administrative costs, and contributions to worker HSAs from business monies. [Estimated work time: 2–4 hours]

(Seeking advice from a competent business tax professional is highly recommended at this stage. You may also wish to review Chapter 7 for tips on where to find deductions for business taxes, and Chapter 8 for advice on integrating HSAs with existing retirement savings plans, and managing any rollover of MSAs or FSAs into HSA accounts.)

____8. Research HSA custodians (banks and other vendors) to manage contributions and withdrawals, if you will be contributing to employee accounts. [Estimated work time: 4–8 hours]

(Review Chapter 4 for tips on selecting custodian vendors. You may wish to compare your existing vendor relationships for other employee retirement benefits (IRAs, 401(k) plans, etc.) with vendors already partnering with your top three insurance picks. If you will be taking the three-step approach, and including HRAs as an interim "cushion" for health savings, you may wish to choose a vendor or vendor partnership with HRA experience.

____9. Make your selection of an insurance policy vendor, HRA vendor (if applicable) and ready a recommended list of HSA account custodians for your employees. [Estimated work time: 1–2 hours]

(If switching insurance vendors, take advantage of the switch by offering fewer options for policy plans. Too many choices often paralyze the decision process, and can slow down adoption of a new concept such as HSAs.)

____10. Set a target launch date and employee-participation goal number for your new benefits plan. You are well on your way to achieving the tax-advantaged benefits of a low-cost and effective health insurance program to help your business grow. The next phase: helping your workers help you reach your business growth goals, by getting them to switching to a more cost-effective health insurance benefit program.

———•◦◦•———

A Health Insurance Glossary

Account Custodian
Bank or other trustee institution which holds funds for an HSA
account holder.

Cafeteria Plan (See Section 125 Plan)

COBRA
An insurance option under U.S. federal law (the Consolidated
Omnibus Budget Reconciliation Act of 1986) that allows
employees who quit, leave, or are fired from a job to continue
coverage under their employer's insurance program, provided the
individual pays the cost of the premiums, for a period of not less
than 18 months.

Catastrophic Care (See Major Medical)

Coinsurance
Shared payment of health care costs, permitted with HSAs only after
a deductible has been met. A typical split is 80/20, with the policyholder paying 20 percent of the fees, and the insurance company paying for the remaining 80 percent directly to the
provider.

Community Rating
A system in several states, including New York State, that skews
health insurance premium costs by city or locality, rather than
the health status or individuals.

Comprehensive Major Medical
Typically an insurance plan that covers basic care as well as major medical coverage and hospitalization.

Co-pay
In an insurance policy, this is the agreed-upon dollar amount an individual will pay on the spot for an office visit, a service, or a prescription; the insurer pays the rest of the fee or charge. Co-pays
are not allowed under HSAs.

Custodial Agreement
The contract between an HSA trustee institution and an account
holder. (See Chapter 4)

Deductible
The agreed-upon amount a policyholder must pay for medical services before the insurer will pick up the tab. Policies may have separate deductibles for in-network and out-of-network providers; under HSAs, only the deductible for in-network providers is considered.

Dependent
For the purposes of this book, a dependent is defined as anyone named as such on an individual or joint personal U.S. tax return, such as a spouse or child.

Disability Insurance
An insurance policy that provides income for someone sick, injured or otherwise unable to work.

Enrollment Period
The deadline period an employee may sign up for an employer based benefits plan.

EPO (Exclusive Provider Organization)
A type of PPO that restricts choice of doctors and services to only those in the plan's network.

Family Deductible
The deductible of a policy, which covers medical expenses of all members of a family, as designated by the policyholder.

FSA (Flexible Spending Account) / FSP (Flexible Spending Plans)
Employee-funded savings plans that pay for health care costs not covered under an employer-based health insurance group plan.

Group Coverage, Group Plan
Insurance for several of individuals under one contract, such as the "group" of employees working for one company, the partners in a business, or members of a trade association or labor union.

High-Deductible Health Insurance (HDHP)
A health insurance policy that requires policyholders to pay more than $1,000 in medical fees, to the limit of the deductible, before the insurer will pay for subsequent care expenses.

HMO (Health Maintenance Organization)
A "prepaid" insurance policy plan that requires participants to use only doctors, hospitals, and other providers affiliated with the plan network. HMOs do not qualify for HSAs.

HRA (Health Reimbursement Account)
An employer-controlled program that reimburses for benefits not covered or otherwise paid for under a company health plan.

HSA (Health Savings Account)
A custodial account specifically used to manage monies for health care expenses, subject to IRS and other federal requirements to be tax-advantaged.

Hospitalization Insurance
Insurance that reimburses for care in a hospital, now not typically sold as a separate policy.

Individual Deductible
The deductible of a policy that covers only the individual named in the policy.

In-Network Provider
A hospital, doctor, or service company affiliated with the insurance policy plan, offering care for a prearranged fee or discount.

Lifetime Maximum or Lifetime Cap
The total amount of costs an insurance policy will pay over the lifetime of the policyholder.

Long-Term Care
Services required for persons with chronic illness, disabilities, or age-related infirmities. Long-term care insurance is a type of policy that reimburses or pays for these services, which may include home attendant care or a nursing home.

Major Medical Insurance
A form of insurance that only covers care for hospitalization and the major costs incurred to treat severe injuries, accidents, or serious illness.

Maternity Benefits
Specific coverage for birth-related medical expenses, which may be an option in a policy.

Medicaid
A medical benefits program administered by states and subsidized by the U.S. federal government, for individuals who meet specific qualifications by law.

MSA (Medical Savings Account)
Also known as Archer Medical Savings Accounts, a federal program discontinued in 2003.

Medicare
The U.S. federal government program, in part funded by payroll taxes, for paying certain hospital and medical expenses for those over 65, and other qualifying individuals. Medicare Part A pays for hospital care; Part B covers other medical expenses.

Medicare Supplemental Insurance
Insurance policies that pay for expenses not covered by Medicare. Medigap is a form of this insurance.

Out-of-Network
A hospital, doctor, or service company not affiliated with the insurance policy plan, which costs may not be covered and/or not included in the deductible limit for that policy.

Out-of-Pocket Costs
Expenses the policyholder must pay for fees and services not covered by an insurance policy, such as coinsurance, usually subject to a maximum cap, after which the insurer will pay other costs.

Permitted Insurance
Other insurance policies in addition to a high-deductible insurance policy that provide health related or work-related benefits, and are allowed with HSAs.

Policy, Policyholder
This is the written and signed contract between an individual (the policyholder) and the insurer, which details payments, reimbursements, coverage inclusions, exclusions, and other matters as agreed to by both parties and a binding legal document.

POS (Point-of-Service)
Any health insurance plan that permits a policyholder to choose either in-network or out-of-network providers.

PPO (Preferred Provider Organization)
A plan that takes its name from the organization (network) of hospitals, doctors and service companies that agree to treat policy-

holders for a set fee or discounted fees. Policyholders typically pay no fees or reduced fees as long as they only use providers "in the network." Some PPOs may qualify for HSAs. (See Chapter 3).

Provider
A health care services supplier, such as a doctor, hospital, clinic, pharmacy, nursing agency, or individual business or company providing health care in exchange for a fee.

Pre-existing Condition
A medical condition known prior to the in-force date of a policy. Typically, policies do not cover expenses for the condition until after a waiting period has been satisfied. The maximum waiting period under federal law is 12 months.

Premium
The common name for the payment given in exchange for coverage under a health care insurance policy, typically paid on a monthly basis to the insurance company.

Preventive Care
Routine care, such as annual health checkups, childhood immunizations, and medical tests designed to discover, treat, or prevent the onset of a more serious medical problem.

Qualified Medical Expenses
For the purpose of this book, qualified medical expenses are expenses that may be considered for tax deduction purposes under IRS rules.

Section 125 Plan
An employee benefits plan, named after its IRS code number, subject to certain federal regulations, which provides a choice of benefits that may be paid for through employee contributions, deducted from pay but tax-free. HSAs may be offered through this type of plan. (Also known as a "cafeteria plan")

Self-Insurance or Self-Funded Plan
Benefits program whereby an employer pays the claims and reimburses for health care, rather than an insurance company.

Workman's Compensation
An insurance program, subject to federal and state regulations, funded by employer taxes, that pays income to employees who become ill or disabled in the workplace.

INDEX

Useful Web Sites

www.HSAfinder.com

The companion website to this book is designed to provide updated sourcing for readers interested in crafting HSA strategies with links here to vendors offering HSA-qualifying health insurance or HSA custodial account products, as well as immediate updates on IRS notices and changes in tax rules.

www.treasury.gov
www.irs.gov

These sites are maintained by the U.S. Treasury Department and the Internal Revenue Service. Notices on tax change rules, updated information on Health Savings Accounts, and downloadable brochures, tax forms, and IRS publications are available here.

www.ama-assn.org

American Medical Association website has many features including patient help information with "Doctor Finder." Group Practic locator, medical specialty society website, state medical society websites, patient education resources, etc.

www.mayoclinic.com

The Mayo Clinic's website offers information on Disease and Conditions A-Z plus Healthy Living, Drugs and Supplements, health tools, etc.

www.nlm.nih.gov
Created by NIH to provides a wide and deep range of health and medical information in books, monographs and online formats.

www.aishealth.com
Atlantic Information Services, Inc. (AIS) is a publishing and information company serving the health care industry.

www.2sbdigest.com
This is the home of Small Business Digest, serving more than one million small and medium-size businesses.

Acknowledgements

This book came about because many individuals approached us asking for a consumer guide. To list them would take too much space. To acknowledge them in this way is our thanks for pointing out a great need that we hope to have fulfilled.

Special thanks again go to the many individuals and business owners who volunteered as examples, and to J. Terence (Terry) MacAvery, CPA, Tax Expert and Attorney-At-Law with Hamilton & MacAvery CPAs, whose expertise and insight proved invaluable in validating financial and tax matters discussed in this book, and to Dr. Kenneth E. Lehrer, economist, for his analysis of HSAs.

Thank you also to the individuals and companies who gave their time and insights, as well as important background material:
John Becker, President, LiveRepair Inc.; Michael Binday, R. Binday Plans & Concepts, Ltd.; Bill Boyles, Edior and Publisher of Consumer Directed Market Repot, Kathryn J. Laing; Sheila Delaney Moroney, National Institute of Health Policy; Peter McCormick, Forest Financial; John O'Leary, VP Market and Business Development, CNA Insurance; Patricia A. M. Riley; Robert G. Romasco; Bill Schaff, Chief Investment Officer, Bay Isle Financial; Mary Lonning Skoy; Martin A. Smith, MetLife Financial Services Strategic Planning Group; William (Bill) J. Thomas, CLU, The PerfectHealth Insurance Company; Mike Vescusco, CHRO, Brocade Communications Systems; and Dr. William J. West, First HSA, Inc.

Other guiding lights whose work influenced my perspective include Senate Majority Leader Bill Frist, M.D. sponsor of the Medicare Prescription Drug, Improvement and Modernization Act (which created Health Savings Accounts) and former Senator Dave Durenberger, Chairman of the National Institute of Health Policy.

Once again, I would like to acknowledge the contributions of my colleagues at Information Strategies, Inc. They and the readers who provided professional support and content, should be credited with helping to shape my thinking and help me to continue to grow as an author. And, my admiration of friends and colleagues, whose own writing successes inspire me.

Finally, my sincere thanks goes to the book team: John T. Colby Jr., Publisher, and his professional staff at Brick Tower Press for recognizing the need to provide information on HSAs; to Donald P. Mazzella for his publishing, editorial and other important collaborations; and, to Elizabeth Bagby for her insights and contributions.

Plus many thanks to my dear friends, professional network and family, you know who you are. Your support is most appreciated!

About the Author

JoAnn Mills Laing has global work and living experience with four public companies (Sara Lee, Olivetti, Chase and Citigroup), as well as running her own successful ecommerce-based businesses. As Chairman of Cybernautics, a premier Audience Development Company, she took the company from idea to profitability and its purchase/IPO (by U.S. Web). She is a graduate of Syracuse University's Whitman School of Management and has an MBA of The Harvard Business School.

As President of Information Strategies, Inc., a marketing and information firm, she has been studying the HSA marketplace. The company, based in Fort Lee, New Jersey, has been regularly polling small firms about health care issues. It also produces online editorial service reaching 1.7 million regular readers each month. She is also the author of *"The Small Business Guide to HSAs."*

For sales, editorial information, subsidiary rights information
or a catalog, please write or phone or e-mail
Brick Tower Press
1230 Park Avenue
New York, NY 10128, US
Sales: 1-800-68-BRICK
Tel: 212-427-7139 Fax: 212-860-8852
www.BrickTowerPress.com
www.bookmanuscript.com
email: bricktower@aol.com.

For Canadian sales please contact our distributor,
Vanwell Publishing Ltd.
1 Northrup Crescent, Box 2131
St. Catharines, ON L2R 7S2
Tel: 905-937-3100

For sales in the UK and Europe please contact our distributor,
Gazelle Book Services
Falcon House, Queens Square
Lancaster, LA1 1RN, UK
Tel: (01524) 68765 Fax: (01524) 63232
email: gazelle4go@aol.com.

For Australian and New Zealand sales please contact
INT Press Distribution Pyt. Ltd.
386 Mt. Alexander Road
Ascot Vale, VIC 3032, Australia
Tel: 61-3-9326 2416 Fax: 61-3-9326 2413
email: sales@intpress.com.au.